Better Homes and Gardens®

Homemade COOKIES

Better Homes and Gardens® Books

Des Moines, Iowa

Copyright © 2000 by Meredith
Corporation, Des Moines, Iowa.
All rights reserved.
Printed in China.
First Edition — 00.
Library of Congress Catalog Card
Number: 00-132137
ISBN: 0-696-21193-9

Pictured on front cover: Chocolate-
Caramel Bars, page 32
Pictured on page 1: Chocolate Chip
Cookies, page 10

Cover photo: D.E. Smith Photography;
Janet Pittman, Food Stylist

Better Homes and Gardens® Books
An imprint of Meredith® Books

Homemade Cookies
Editor: Jennifer Dorland Darling
Contributing Editors: Shelli McConnell, Mary Major Williams
Associate Art Director: Lynda Haupert
Copy Chief: Catherine Hamrick
Copy and Production Editor: Terri Fredrickson
Managers, Book Production: Pam Kvitne, Marjorie J. Schenkelberg
Contributing Copy Editor: Kim Catanzarite
Contributing Proofreaders: Kathy Eastman, Gretchen Kauffman,
    James A. Stepp
Indexer: Kathleen Poole
Electronic Production Coordinator: Paula Forest
Editorial and Design Assistants: Judy Bailey, Mary Lee Gavin,
    Karen Schirm
Test Kitchen Director: Lynn Blanchard
Test Kitchen Home Economists: Patricia Beebout, Judy Comstock,
    Marilyn Cornelius, Maryellyn Krantz, Tammy Leonard, Jan Miller,
    R.D., Jill Moberly, Dianna Nolin, Jennifer Peterson, Kay Springer,
    Colleen Weeden, Lori Wilson, Charles Worthington

Meredith® Books
Editor in Chief: James D. Blume
Design Director: Matt Strelecki
Managing Editor: Gregory H. Kayko

Director, Retail Sales and Marketing: Terry Unsworth
Director, Sales, Special Markets: Rita McMullen
Director, Sales, Premiums: Michael A. Peterson
Director, Sales, Retail: Tom Wierzbicki
Director, Sales, Home & Garden Centers: Ray Wolf
Director, Book Marketing: Brad Elmitt
Director, Operations: George A. Susral
Director, Production: Douglas M. Johnston

Vice President, General Manager: Jamie L. Martin

Better Homes and Gardens® Magazine
Editor in Chief: Jean LemMon
Executive Food Editor: Nancy Byal

Meredith Publishing Group
President, Publishing Group: Christopher M. Little
Vice President, Finance & Administration: Max Runciman

Meredith Corporation
Chairman and Chief Executive Officer: William T. Kerr

Chairman of the Executive Committee: E. T. Meredith III

Contents

Substitution Chart
(see inside back cover)

Welcome to Our Kitchen

When you cook with a Better Homes and Gardens® cookbook, you can be confident that every recipe will taste great every time. That's because we perfect every recipe in our Test Kitchen before we share them with you.

Isn't it fun to stop by a friend's house for a cup of coffee and a freshly baked cookie so wonderful you have to have the recipe?

Think of the Home Economists in the Better Homes and Gardens® Test Kitchen as good friends who can't wait to share their cookie recipes and tips with you. When you open this cookbook, imagine you're dropping by our kitchen—just as you would a friend's for coffee and cookies.

In fact, each of our kitchens is equipped with standard ovens, mixers, and other appliances just like those in your kitchen. And, like you, we purchase groceries at neighborhood supermarkets in family-size packages and portions.

Our daily routine, however, is different. We pull a lot of kitchen duty so you don't have to. Before we don our aprons and roll up our sleeves, we review the details of every recipe. Are the baking time and temperature correct? Can we offer raisins as an option to chocolate pieces? Can the mixing be simplified?

By the time we start measuring flour, we have a pretty good idea of how the cookie will come together, but we may find that the steps that look great on paper fail to work in reality. That's when the Home Economist calls on her knowledge and experience to modify a technique, adjust a baking time, or alter a spice level.

Then comes the time to nibble, which is always the best part. For taste panel, we gather around the table, tasting cookies and talking over what works and what doesn't. Once the recipe is revised, the process begins again. We refine and tweak the recipe until everyone agrees that the cookie is 100 percent perfect.

Every step of the way, we look for ways to make the recipe faster, easier to use, and better tasting. Our goal is simple: to provide you with cookie recipes that taste delicious, work every time, and that your family will ask for again and again.

Lynn Blanchard

Enjoy!
Lynn Blanchard
Test Kitchen Director

Secrets to Success

Cookie questions? No problem! The Home Economists in the Better Homes and Gardens® Test Kitchen solve baking problems every day. Here are answers to the most commonly asked questions concerning cookies that we have received from cooks across the country.

Q.

Do I need to sift the flour when making cookies?

A.

Thanks to advances in flour production, for most recipes, it's no longer necessary to sift flour. However, measuring flour accurately is critical to the success of your cookies. Always measure flour with nested metal or plastic cups. Glass or plastic cups with graduated measurements on the sides and spouts are meant for liquids. If you use a liquid measuring cup for flour, you could end up with an extra tablespoon or more per cup. Begin by stirring the flour while it is still in the container. Using a large spoon, gently spoon the flour into the measuring cup and level off the top with the straight edge of a metal spatula. Do not pack the flour into the cup or tap it to level it.

Q.

Can I mix cookie dough with a handheld portable mixer or do I need a stand mixer?

A.

Most cookie recipes, and all of the recipes in this book, can be made with a portable mixer although you may need to work a little harder. Most portable mixers are less powerful than stand mixers, so when it comes to adding the last of the flour, you'll need to stir it in with a wooden spoon. Whether you're using a portable or a stand mixer, begin stirring in the flour by hand once the mixer starts to strain.

Q.

How long can I store cookies?

A.

Store baked cookies for up to 3 days in a tightly covered container. For longer storage, freeze them for up to 3 months. Since cookies are small, they thaw quickly and will be ready to eat in 15 minutes. For the best results, freeze cookies unfrosted or unadorned with chocolate dips or drizzles. Frost, dip, or drizzle the cookies after they thaw.

Q.

What cookie sheets work best for baking cookies?

A.

Look for shiny, heavy gauge cookie sheets with very low or no sides. Avoid dark cookie sheets; they may cause cookie bottoms to overbrown. Use jelly-roll pans (15×10×1-inch baking pans) only for bar cookies. Other types of cookies will not bake evenly in a pan with an edge. If you must use such a pan, turn it over and bake cookies on the bottom.

Insulated cookie sheets tend to yield pale cookies with soft centers. You may have trouble using them for cookies containing a large amount of butter, such as shortbread, because the butter may melt and leak out before the dough is set. Do not bake cookies on insulated cookie sheets long enough to brown on the bottom because the rest of the cookies may become too dry.

Q.

Why do my cookies always seem to require an extra minute or two of baking time?

A.

First, check your oven with an oven thermometer to be sure it's working correctly. If the thermometer registers lower than the setting, increase the oven temperature accordingly. If the thermometer registers the correct temperature, bake the cookies a minute or two longer. You may have used more dough per cookie resulting in larger cookies that will take longer to bake.

Q.

What makes cookies hard and tough?

A.

Cookies become hard when they are overbaked. Check the oven temperature with an oven thermometer and reduce the temperature, if needed. If the temperature is correct, reduce the baking time 1 to 2 minutes. Another reason for hard cookies is overmixing the dough. After adding the flour, mix just until combined. And be sure you've measured the flour correctly. Too much flour causes cookies to be tough.

Q.

Why are some of the cookies perfectly done while others are doughy and some are too brown?

A.

To ensure even baking, use a cookie sheet that fits in the oven with at least 1 inch to spare all around. Bake only one cookie sheet at a time, and be sure the rack is in the middle of the oven. Be careful to place the cookies on the cookie sheet exactly as specified in the recipe. The spacing has been worked out to allow for spreading of the dough and even airflow around the cookies.

better with butter

Which makes better cookies—butter or margarine?

All of the recipes in *Homemade Cookies* call for butter. Butter gives a wonderful flavor and ensures good results. Many margarines contain more water than oil and will yield undesirable results. If you wish to use margarine instead of butter, use only stick margarine that contains at least 60 to 80 percent vegetable oil (oil content is listed on the package). Margarines will produce a softer dough, so you may need to chill it longer than directed. Soft, spreadable margarines have a high water content and can cause cookies to be tough and to dry out faster.

Drop Cookies

Cashew Meringues

In this Chapter:

Ranger Cookies

Two essential ingredients earmark this classic—crisp rice cereal and sweet, chewy coconut. These crisp cookies make a great treat to tuck into a brown-bag lunch.

Prep: 25 minutes   **Bake:** 8 minutes   **Oven:** 375°   **Makes:** 54

½ cup butter, softened
½ cup granulated sugar
½ cup packed brown sugar
½ teaspoon baking powder
¼ teaspoon baking soda
1 egg
1 teaspoon vanilla
1¼ cups all-purpose flour
2 cups crisp rice cereal or
    1 cup rolled oats
1 3½-ounce can (1⅓ cups)
    flaked coconut
1 cup snipped pitted whole
    dates or raisins

1 In a medium mixing bowl beat butter with an electric mixer on medium to high speed for 30 seconds. Add granulated sugar, brown sugar, baking powder, and baking soda; beat until combined, scraping sides of bowl occasionally. Beat in egg and vanilla until combined. Beat in as much of the flour as you can with the mixer. Using a wooden spoon, stir in any remaining flour. Stir in cereal or oats, coconut, and dates or raisins. Drop by rounded teaspoons 2 inches apart onto ungreased cookie sheet.

2 Bake in a 375° oven about 8 minutes or until edges are golden brown. Cool on cookie sheet for 1 minute. Transfer cookies to a wire rack; cool.

Nutrition Facts per cookie: 61 cal., 2 g total fat (2 g sat. fat), 8 mg chol., 40 mg sodium, 10 g carbo., 1 g fiber, 1 g pro.

To Make Ahead: Bake cookies as directed and cool completely. Place in a freezer container or bag and freeze up to 3 months. Before serving, thaw cookies about 15 minutes.

kids and cookies

Kids love cookies—they love to eat them, and they love to make them. So next time you and your child have a free hour or two, mix up a batch of cookie dough and share some magical moments in the kitchen. Any child old enough to pull a chair up to the counter is ready to make cookies. Young children can add ingredients to the bowl, and you can take care of the mixing. Older children can measure the ingredients and mix the dough while you stand back and supervise.

Not yet bound by the rules of convention, children bring a unique perspective to cookie-making. You may carefully follow the directions for shaping the dough and decorating cookies, but children bring their own ideas to a recipe. Let them shape the dough into snakes, spiders, or any other creatures they desire. For most kids, decorating cookies is the best part, so provide plenty of options such as frostings, candies, dried fruit, and sprinkles. Let the kids choose the colors to tint the frosting. They probably have a design in mind—maybe something special for Mom or Dad. And as you pack up the baked and decorated cookies, savor the moment. After all, they're children for such a short time.

Oatmeal Cookies Three Ways

From one cookie dough, you can make three different kinds of cookies. Or, mix up the whole batch as one variation—simply triple the ingredients listed for that variation.

Prep: 25 minutes **Bake:** 9 to 11 minutes **Oven:** 375° **Makes:** 96

1½ cups butter, softened
2 cups packed brown sugar
1 cup granulated sugar
2 teaspoons baking powder
½ teaspoon baking soda
2 eggs
¼ cup milk
2 teaspoons vanilla
3¾ cups all-purpose flour
2 cups rolled oats

1 In an extra-large mixing bowl beat butter with an electric mixer on medium to high speed for 30 seconds. Add brown sugar, granulated sugar, baking powder, and baking soda; beat until combined, scraping sides of bowl occasionally. Beat in eggs, milk, and vanilla until combined. Beat in as much of the flour as you can with the mixer. Using a wooden spoon, stir in any remaining flour and the rolled oats.

2 Divide dough into three equal portions. Choose one of the variations below to add to each portion of dough. Drop by rounded teaspoons 2 inches apart onto ungreased cookie sheet.

3 Bake in a 375° oven for 9 to 11 minutes or until edges are golden, but centers are soft. Cool on the cookie sheet for 1 minute. Transfer cookies to a wire rack; cool.

Nutrition Facts per cookie: 235 cal., 10 g total fat (6 g sat. fat), 38 mg chol., 148 mg sodium, 34 g carbo., 1 g fiber, 2 g pro.

Spicy Raisin Rounds: Stir in 1 cup raisins or currants, 1 teaspoon ground cinnamon, and ¼ teaspoon ground cloves. Continue as directed.

Nutrition Facts per cookie: 249 cal., 10 g total fat (6 g sat. fat), 38 mg chol., 149 mg sodium, 38 g carbo., 1 g fiber, 3 g pro.

Nutty Brickle Chippers: Stir in 1 cup chopped chocolate-covered English toffee or semisweet chocolate pieces and ½ cup chopped walnuts or hazelnuts (filberts). Continue as directed.

Nutrition Facts per cookie: 273 cal., 13 g total fat (7 g sat. fat), 38 mg chol., 149 mg sodium, 36 g carbo., 2 g fiber, 3 g pro.

Candy Cookies: Stir in 1 cup snipped or chopped gumdrops or candy-coated milk chocolate pieces. Continue as directed.

Nutrition Facts per cookie: 257 cal., 10 g total fat (6 g sat. fat), 38 mg chol., 151 mg sodium, 40 g carbo., 1 g fiber, 3 g pro.

Chocolate Chip Cookies

A cookie book just wouldn't be complete without these all-time favorites. This recipe is an updated version of one that first appeared in the 1941 edition of the Better Homes and Gardens® Cookbook.

Prep: 25 minutes **Bake:** 8 to 10 minutes **Oven:** 375° **Makes:** 60

½ cup shortening
½ cup butter, softened
1 cup packed brown sugar
½ cup granulated sugar
½ teaspoon baking soda
2 eggs
1 teaspoon vanilla
2½ cups all-purpose flour
1 12-ounce package
   (2 cups) semisweet
   chocolate pieces
1½ cups chopped walnuts,
   pecans, or hazelnuts
   (optional)

1 In a large mixing bowl beat shortening and butter with an electric mixer on medium to high speed for 30 seconds. Add brown sugar, granulated sugar, and baking soda; beat until combined, scraping sides of bowl occasionally. Beat in eggs and vanilla until combined. Beat in as much of the flour as you can with the mixer. Using a wooden spoon, stir in any remaining flour. Stir in chocolate pieces and, if desired, nuts.

2 Drop dough by rounded teaspoons 2 inches apart onto an ungreased cookie sheet.

3 Bake in a 375° oven for 8 to 10 minutes or until edges are lightly browned. Transfer cookies to a wire rack; cool.

Nutrition Facts per cookie: 98 cal., 5 g total fat (2 g sat. fat), 11 mg chol., 30 mg sodium, 11 g carbo., 1 g fiber, 1 g pro.

Macadamia Nut and White Chocolate Cookies: Prepare as directed, except substitute chopped white baking bars or white chocolate baking squares for the semisweet chocolate pieces. Stir in one 3½-ounce jar macadamia nuts, chopped, with the chopped white baking bars or squares.

Nutrition Facts per cookie: 96 cal., 7 g total fat (3 g sat. fat), 12 mg chol., 37 mg sodium, 9 g carbo., 0 g fiber, 1 g pro.

To Make Ahead: Bake cookies as directed and cool completely. Place in a freezer container or bag and freeze up to 3 months. Before serving, thaw cookies about 15 minutes.

Cashew-Chocolate Drops

Your blender or food processor makes quick work of grinding the cashews. For evenly ground nuts, add about ¼ cup of the flour with the cashews and pulse the blender or processor on and off.

Prep: 25 minutes   **Bake:** 10 to 12 minutes   **Oven:** 350°   **Makes:** 48

½ cup butter, softened
1 cup packed brown sugar
1 teaspoon baking powder
¼ teaspoon baking soda
1 egg
1 teaspoon finely shredded lemon peel
2 tablespoons lemon juice
1 teaspoon vanilla
1¾ cups all-purpose flour
1 cup cashews, ground
1 cup semisweet chocolate pieces

1 In a large mixing bowl beat butter with an electric mixer on medium to high speed for 30 seconds. Add brown sugar, baking powder, and baking soda; beat until combined, scraping sides of bowl occasionally. Beat in egg, lemon peel, lemon juice, and vanilla until combined. Using a wooden spoon, stir in flour, ground cashews, and chocolate pieces.

2 Drop dough by rounded teaspoons 2 inches apart onto an ungreased cookie sheet.

3 Bake in a 350° oven for 10 to 12 minutes or until edges are lightly browned. Cool on cookie sheet for 1 minute. Transfer cookies to a wire rack; cool.

Nutrition Facts per cookie: 86 cal., 4 g total fat (2 g sat. fat), 10 mg chol., 39 mg sodium, 10 g carbo., 1 g fiber, 1 g pro.

To Make Ahead: Bake cookies as directed and cool completely. Place in a freezer container or bag and freeze up to 3 months. Before serving, thaw cookies about 15 minutes.

make-ahead dough

Crunched for time but still longing to treat your family to fresh-baked cookies? Get over your guilt and beat the clock by mixing the dough ahead of time.

To mix the dough ahead, prepare as directed, cover, and chill for up to 24 hours. The dough will become firm with chilling, so before using let it stand at room temperature until it returns to its just-mixed consistency. For longer storage, pack the dough into freezer containers and freeze for up to one month. When ready to bake the cookies, thaw the dough for several hours in the refrigerator.

Colleen Weeden
Test Kitchen Home Economist

Peanut Butter and Oatmeal Rounds

How do you improve upon a classic? Combine three timeless favorites—chocolate chip, oatmeal, and peanut butter—in one sumptuous cookie.

Prep: 20 minutes **Bake:** 10 minutes **Oven:** 375° **Makes:** 60

¾ cup butter, softened
½ cup peanut butter
1 cup granulated sugar
½ cup packed brown sugar
1 teaspoon baking powder
½ teaspoon baking soda
2 eggs
1 teaspoon vanilla
1¼ cups all-purpose flour
2 cups rolled oats
1 cup semisweet chocolate
    pieces (6 ounces)

1 In a large mixing bowl beat butter and peanut butter with an electric mixer on medium to high speed for 30 seconds. Add granulated sugar, brown sugar, baking powder, and baking soda; beat until combined, scraping sides of bowl occasionally. Beat in eggs and vanilla until combined. Beat in as much of the flour as you can with the mixer. Using a wooden spoon, stir in any remaining flour, oats, and chocolate pieces.

2 Drop dough from rounded teaspoons 2 inches apart onto an ungreased cookie sheet.

3 Bake in a 375° oven about 10 minutes or until edges are lightly browned. Transfer cookies to a wire rack; cool.

Nutrition Facts per cookie: 92 cal., 5 g total fat (2 g sat. fat), 14 mg chol., 55 mg sodium, 10 g carbo., 1 g fiber, 1 g pro.

To Make Ahead: Bake cookies as directed and cool completely. Place in a freezer container or bag and freeze up to 3 months. Before serving, thaw cookies about 15 minutes.

any-occasion gifts

Home-baked cookies make wonderful gifts for just about any occasion. To give the gift a special touch, pack the cookies in a decorative gift box or tin lined with colored tissue paper. Wrap the cookies individually or in pairs in clear plastic wrap before packing them in the box. Leave the box open to showcase the cookies or cover it with the lid to keep the contents a surprise. Finish the package by tying sheer ribbon around the top or sides of the box.

Jumbo Oatmeal Cookies

Oat flour gives these oversize cookies a finer texture than traditional oatmeal cookies. Use your blender or food processor to grind rolled oats into oat flour and to finely chop the coconut.

Prep: 25 minutes   **Bake:** 13 to 15 minutes   **Oven:** 350°   **Makes:** 36

2 cups rolled oats
⅓ cup flaked coconut
⅓ cup butter, softened
⅓ cup shortening
¾ cup granulated sugar
¾ cup packed brown sugar
1 teaspoon baking soda
2 eggs
1 teaspoon vanilla
1 cup all-purpose flour
1 cup coarsely chopped walnuts
1 cup chocolate-covered raisins

1 For oat flour, place ½ cup oats in a blender container or 1 cup oats in a food processor bowl. Cover and blend or process until oats turn into a powder. Transfer the powder to a small bowl. Repeat with remaining oats, working with ½ to 1 cup oats at a time. Set aside.

2 Place coconut in blender container or food processor bowl. Cover and blend or process until coconut is very finely chopped. Set aside.

3 In a large mixing bowl beat butter and shortening with an electric mixer on medium to high speed for 30 seconds. Add the granulated sugar, brown sugar, and soda. Beat until combined, scraping sides of bowl occasionally. Beat in eggs and vanilla until combined. Beat in oat flour, coconut, and as much of the all-purpose flour as you can with the mixer. Using a wooden spoon, stir in any remaining flour. Stir in the walnuts and raisins.

4 Drop dough by a ¼-cup measure about 4 inches apart onto an ungreased cookie sheet.

5 Bake cookies in a 350° oven for 13 to 15 minutes or until the edges are golden brown. Cool on cookie sheet for 1 minute. Transfer cookies to a wire rack; cool.

Nutrition Facts per cookie: 147 cal., 7 g total fat (3 g sat. fat), 17 mg chol., 61 mg sodium, 19 g carbo., 1 g fiber, 2 g pro.

To make standard-size cookies: Drop the dough by rounded teaspoons 2 inches apart on an ungreased cookie sheet. Bake in a 350° oven for 8 to 10 minutes or until the edges are lightly browned. Transfer cookies to a wire rack; cool. Makes 108.

Nutrition Facts per cookie: 49 cal., 2 g total fat (1 g sat. fat), 6 mg chol., 20 mg sodium, 6 g carbo., 0 g fiber, 1 g pro.

To Make Ahead: Bake cookies as directed and cool completely. Place in a freezer container or bag and freeze up to 3 months. Before serving, thaw cookies about 15 minutes.

Frosted Butterscotch Cookies

Browning butter is a technique for bestowing a rich, toasty flavor to baked foods. Here it imparts a golden color and luscious flavor to the velvety frosting that cloaks these brown sugar gems.

Prep: 25 minutes **Bake:** 10 to 12 minutes **Oven:** 375° **Makes:** 60

2½ cups all-purpose flour
½ teaspoon salt
1 teaspoon baking soda
½ teaspoon baking powder
1½ cups packed brown sugar
½ cup shortening
2 eggs
1 teaspoon vanilla
1 8-ounce carton dairy sour cream
⅔ cup chopped walnuts
1 recipe Browned Butter Frosting
Walnut halves or chopped walnuts (optional)

1 Lightly grease a cookie sheet; set aside. In a medium bowl stir together flour, salt, baking soda, and baking powder; set aside.

2 In a large mixing bowl beat brown sugar and shortening with an electric mixer on medium to high speed until well mixed. Add eggs and vanilla. Beat until combined. Add flour mixture and sour cream alternately to beaten mixture, beating after each addition. Stir in chopped walnuts.

3 Drop dough by rounded teaspoons 2 inches apart onto the prepared cookie sheet.

4 Bake in a 375° oven for 10 to 12 minutes or until edges are light brown. Transfer to a wire rack; cool completely. Spread cooled cookies with Browned Butter Frosting. If desired, top with walnut halves or additional chopped walnuts.

Browned Butter Frosting: In a medium saucepan heat and stir ½ cup butter over medium-low heat until golden brown. (Do not scorch.) Remove from heat. Stir in 3½ cups sifted powdered sugar, 5 teaspoons boiling water, and 1½ teaspoons vanilla. Beat until frosting is easy to spread. Immediately spread on cookies. If frosting begins to set up, stir in a small amount of additional boiling water.

Nutrition Facts per cookie: 105 cal., 5 g total fat (2 g sat. fat), 13 mg chol., 63 mg sodium, 14 g carbo., 0 g fiber, 1 g pro.

To Make Ahead: Bake and cool cookies as directed, but do not frost. Place in a freezer container or bag and freeze up to 3 months. Thaw cookies about 15 minutes. Prepare frosting and spread over thawed cookies.

Ultimate Chocolate Cookies

With fudgy centers, chocolate pieces, nuts, and a drizzle of chocolate, it's plain to see how these cookies came by their name. Any doubts? Bake up a batch and see for yourself.

Prep: 30 minutes   **Bake:** 8 to 10 minutes   **Oven:** 350°   **Makes:** 36

1   12-ounce package
      (2 cups) semisweet
      chocolate pieces
2   ounces unsweetened
      chocolate
2   tablespoons butter
¼   cup all-purpose flour
¼   teaspoon baking powder
      Dash salt
2   eggs
⅔   cup granulated sugar
1   teaspoon vanilla
1   cup chopped nuts
4   ounces semisweet
      chocolate, melted

1 Lightly grease a cookie sheet; set aside. Melt 1 cup of the semisweet chocolate pieces, the unsweetened chocolate, and butter in a heavy medium saucepan, stirring constantly. Transfer to large mixing bowl; cool slightly. Meanwhile, stir together flour, baking powder, and salt; set aside. Add eggs, sugar, and vanilla to chocolate mixture. Using a wooden spoon, beat until combined. Stir in the flour mixture, remaining chocolate pieces, and nuts. Drop dough by heaping teaspoons 2 inches apart onto the prepared cookie sheet.

2 Bake in a 350° oven for 8 to 10 minutes or until edges are firm and surface is dull and cracked. Cool on cookie sheet for 1 minute. Transfer to a wire rack; cool completely. Drizzle cooled cookies with melted semisweet chocolate.

Nutrition Facts per cookie: 118 cal., 7 g total fat (3 g sat. fat), 14 mg chol., 18 mg sodium, 9 g carbo., 2 g fiber, 1 g pro.

To Make Ahead: Bake and cool cookies as directed, but do not drizzle with chocolate. Place in a freezer container and freeze up to 3 months. Thaw cookies 15 minutes; drizzle with chocolate.

dazzle with a drizzle

A drizzle of melted chocolate or candy coating can be just the thing to finish off your cookies in style. Here are some suggestions to ensure dazzling results.

Place the cookies on a wire rack over waxed paper. Dip a fork into the melted chocolate or candy coating, letting the first clumpy bit land in the pan; then pass the fork over the cookies, letting the chocolate drizzle off. For added color, melt tinted candy coating. Or, tint melted white baking bar or candy coating with paste food coloring. Do not use liquid food coloring. The liquid in the coloring will cause white baking bar to separate and curdle.

Frosted Sour Cream-Chocolate Drops

Swirls of chocolate buttercream frosting top these deep chocolate delights. A plate of them covered with plastic wrap and graced with a bow makes a sure-to-please gift for a chocolate-loving friend.

Prep: 30 minutes   **Bake:** 8 to 10 minutes   **Oven:** 350°   **Makes:** 42

½ cup butter, softened
1 cup packed brown sugar
½ teaspoon baking soda
¼ teaspoon salt
1 egg
1 teaspoon vanilla
2 ounces unsweetened chocolate, melted and cooled
1 8-ounce carton dairy sour cream
2 cups all-purpose flour
1 recipe Chocolate Butter Frosting

1 In a large mixing bowl beat butter with an electric mixer on medium to high speed for 30 seconds. Add brown sugar, baking soda, and salt; beat until combined, scraping sides of bowl occasionally. Beat in egg and vanilla. Add melted chocolate; beat until combined. Beat in sour cream. Beat in as much of the flour as you can with the mixer. Using a wooden spoon, stir in any remaining flour.

2 Drop dough by slightly rounded teaspoons 2 inches apart onto an ungreased cookie sheet.

3 Bake in a 350° oven for 8 to 10 minutes or until edges are firm. Transfer cookies to a wire rack; cool completely. Spread cooled cookies with Chocolate Butter Frosting.

Chocolate Butter Frosting: In a medium mixing bowl beat ¼ cup butter until fluffy. Gradually add 1 cup sifted powdered sugar and ⅓ cup unsweetened cocoa powder, beating well. Slowly beat in 3 tablespoons milk and 1 teaspoon vanilla. Slowly beat in an additional 1½ cups sifted powdered sugar. If necessary, beat in additional milk to make frosting of spreading consistency.

Nutrition Facts per cookie: 111 cal., 5 g total fat (3 g sat. fat), 16 mg chol., 67 mg sodium, 15 g carbo., 0 g fiber, 1 g pro.

To Make Ahead: Bake and cool cookies as directed, but do not frost. Place in a freezer container or bag and freeze up to 3 months. Thaw cookies about 15 minutes. Prepare frosting and spread over thawed cookies.

White Chocolate-Raspberry Cookies

With a festive white chocolate drizzle and bright raspberry filling, these cookies are perfect fare for a graduation, a shower, or a special open house.

Prep: 30 minutes **Bake:** 7 to 9 minutes **Oven:** 375° **Makes:** 48

    8 ounces white baking bar
    ½ cup butter, softened
    1 cup granulated sugar
    1 teaspoon baking soda
    ¼ teaspoon salt
    2 eggs
 2¾ cups all-purpose flour
    ½ cup seedless raspberry jam
    3 ounces white baking bar
    ½ teaspoon shortening

1 Lightly grease a cookie sheet; set aside. Chop 4 ounces of the white baking bar; set aside. In a heavy small saucepan, melt the remaining 4 ounces of the white baking bar over low heat while stirring constantly; cool.

2 In a large mixing bowl beat butter with an electric mixer on medium to high speed for 30 seconds. Add sugar, baking soda, and salt; beat until combined, scraping sides of bowl occasionally. Beat in eggs and the melted white baking bar until combined. Beat in as much of the flour as you can with the mixer. Using a wooden spoon, stir in any remaining flour. Stir in the chopped white baking bar.

3 Drop dough by rounded teaspoons 2 inches apart onto the prepared cookie sheet.

4 Bake in a 375° oven for 7 to 9 minutes or until edges are lightly browned. Cool on cookie sheet for 1 minute. Transfer to a wire rack; cool completely.

5 Just before serving, in a small saucepan melt the raspberry jam over low heat. Spoon about ½ teaspoon of the jam onto the top of each cookie. In a heavy, small saucepan combine the 3 ounces white baking bar and shortening. Melt over low heat, stirring constantly. Drizzle each cookie with some of the melted mixture. If necessary, refrigerate about 15 minutes to firm baking bar mixture.

Nutrition Facts per cookie: 104 cal., 4 g total fat (2 g sat. fat), 14 mg chol., 66 mg sodium, 16 g carbo., 0 g fiber, 1 g pro.

To Make Ahead: Bake and cool cookies as directed, but do not top with jam or white chocolate drizzle. Place in a freezer container and freeze up to 3 months. Thaw cookies, top with jam, and drizzle with white chocolate as directed.

Cashew Meringues

Crisp and delicate on the outside with melt-in-your-mouth centers, meringue cookies are a delightful melding of textures. Melted caramels make a luscious drizzle.

Prep: 25 minutes   **Bake:** 15 minutes   **Oven:** 325°   **Makes:** 60

  4 egg whites
  1 teaspoon vanilla
  ¼ teaspoon cream of tartar
  4 cups sifted powdered
      sugar
  2 cups chopped cashews or
      mixed nuts
 12 vanilla caramels
  2 teaspoons milk
      Chopped cashews or
          mixed nuts (optional)

1 In a large mixing bowl allow egg whites to stand at room temperature for 30 minutes. Meanwhile, lightly grease a cookie sheet; set aside.

2 Add vanilla and cream of tartar to egg whites. Beat with an electric mixer on medium speed until soft peaks form (tips curl). Gradually add the powdered sugar, about ¼ cup at a time, beating on medium speed just until combined. Beat for 1 to 2 minutes more or until soft peaks form. (Do not continue beating to stiff peaks.) Using a spoon, gently fold in the 2 cups cashews or mixed nuts.

3 Drop egg white mixture by rounded teaspoons 2 inches apart onto prepared cookie sheet.

4 Bake in a 325° oven 15 minutes or until edges are very light brown. Transfer cookies to a wire rack; cool completely.

5 In a small saucepan combine the caramels and milk. Heat and stir over low heat until the caramels are melted. Place cookies on a wire rack over waxed paper. Drizzle caramel mixture over cookies. If desired, sprinkle with additional chopped cashews or mixed nuts. Let stand until caramel mixture is set.

Nutrition Facts per cookie: 61 cal., 2 g total fat (1 g sat. fat), 0 mg chol., 9 mg sodium, 10 g carbo., 0 g fiber, 1 g pro.

To Make Ahead: Bake and cool cookies as directed, but do not drizzle with caramel mixture. Place in a freezer container and freeze up to 3 months. Thaw cookies; drizzle with caramel mixture and sprinkle with nuts as directed.

Orange Snowdrops

A can of frozen orange juice concentrate imparts a sunshine-fresh flavor to these cookies. Use half of the can in the cookie dough and the remaining concentrate in the frosting.

Prep: 25 minutes **Bake:** 8 minutes **Oven:** 375° **Makes:** 36

½ cup butter, softened
½ cup shortening
1 cup sifted powdered sugar
½ teaspoon baking soda
1 egg
½ of a 6-ounce can (⅓ cup) frozen orange juice concentrate, thawed
1 teaspoon vanilla
2 cups all-purpose flour
1 recipe Orange Frosting
   Finely shredded orange peel (optional)

1 In a large mixing bowl beat butter and shortening with an electric mixer on medium to high speed for 30 seconds. Add powdered sugar and soda; beat until combined, scraping sides of bowl occasionally. Beat in egg, juice concentrate, and vanilla until combined. Beat in as much of the flour as you can with the mixer. Using a wooden spoon, stir in any remaining flour.

2 Drop dough by rounded teaspoons 2 inches apart onto an ungreased cookie sheet.

3 Bake in a 375° oven about 8 minutes or until edges are lightly browned. Cool on cookie sheet for 1 minute. Transfer cookies to a wire rack; cool completely. Spread cooled cookies with Orange Frosting. If desired, sprinkle frosted cookies with finely shredded orange peel.

Orange Frosting: In a medium mixing bowl stir together half of a 6-ounce can (⅓ cup) frozen orange juice concentrate, thawed; ½ teaspoon finely shredded orange peel; and 3 cups sifted powdered sugar until smooth.

Nutrition Facts per cookie: 129 cal., 6 g total fat (2 g sat. fat), 13 mg chol., 47 mg sodium, 18 g carbo., 0 g fiber, 1 g pro.

To Make Ahead: Bake and cool cookies as directed, but do not frost. Place in a freezer container or bag and freeze up to 3 months. Thaw cookies about 15 minutes. Prepare frosting and spread over thawed cookies.

Chewy Coconut Macaroons

Moist and fluffy macaroons were all the rage in Paris 100 years ago. This almond-scented, coconut version makes it easy to see why.

Prep: 15 minutes   **Bake:** 20 to 25 minutes   **Oven:** 325°   **Makes:** 30

2   3½-ounce cans (2⅔ cups total) flaked coconut
⅔   cup granulated sugar
⅓   cup all-purpose flour
¼   teaspoon salt
4   egg whites
½   teaspoon almond extract
2   ounces semisweet chocolate (optional)
½   teaspoon shortening (optional)

1 Lightly grease and flour a large cookie sheet; set aside. In a medium bowl combine coconut, sugar, flour, and salt. Stir in egg whites and almond extract.

2 Drop egg white mixture by rounded teaspoons 2 inches apart onto prepared cookie sheet.

3 Bake in a 325° oven for 20 to 25 minutes or until edges are golden brown. Transfer cookies to a wire rack; cool completely. If desired, in a heavy small saucepan melt chocolate and shortening; drizzle over cooled cookies.

Nutrition Facts per cookie: 54 cal., 2 g total fat (2 g sat. fat), 0 mg chol., 26 mg sodium, 8 g carbo., 0 g fiber, 1 g pro.

To Make Ahead: Bake and cool as directed; do not drizzle with chocolate. Place in a freezer container or bag and freeze up to 3 months. Thaw cookies 15 minutes and drizzle with chocolate.

macaroons vs. meringues

Macaroons often get confused with meringue cookies, but there is a difference. Although both are made with egg whites, the similarity ends there. Macaroons are chewy and may contain ground nuts, almond paste, or coconut. Meringue cookies contain egg whites and sugar. The meringue mixture is beaten until stiff and baked until crisp. For a meringue-style cookie, try Cashew Meringues on page 19.

Lemon Drops

A simple glaze of sugar and lemon juice lends sparkle to these dainty treats. Enjoy their tangy lemon flavor with a cup of hot tea.

Prep: 25 minutes   **Bake:** 8 minutes   **Oven:** 375°   **Makes:** 36

½ cup butter, softened
¾ cup granulated sugar
4 teaspoons finely shredded
   lemon peel
½ teaspoon baking powder
½ teaspoon baking soda
⅛ teaspoon salt
1 egg
½ cup dairy sour cream
⅓ cup lemon juice
2 cups all-purpose flour
1 recipe Lemon Glaze

1 In a large mixing bowl beat butter with an electric mixer on medium to high speed for 30 seconds. Add sugar, lemon peel, baking powder, baking soda, and salt. Beat until combined, scraping sides of bowl. Beat in egg, sour cream, and lemon juice until combined. Beat in as much of the flour as you can with the mixer. Using a wooden spoon, stir in any remaining flour.

2 Drop dough by slightly rounded tablespoons 3 inches apart onto an ungreased cookie sheet.

3 Bake in a 375° oven about 8 minutes or until tops are firm. Transfer the cookies to a wire rack. Brush the tops of warm cookies with Lemon Glaze; cool.

Lemon Glaze: In a small mixing bowl stir together ¼ cup granulated sugar and 2 tablespoons lemon juice.

Nutrition Facts per cookie: 72 cal., 4 g total fat (1 g sat. fat), 11 mg chol., 57 mg sodium, 9 g carbo., 0 g fiber, 1 g pro.

To Make Ahead: Bake and cool cookies as directed, but do not glaze. Place in a freezer container or bag and freeze up to 3 months. Thaw cookies about 15 minutes. Prepare glaze and brush over thawed cookies.

Brownies & Bars

Toasted Hazelnut Bars

In this Chapter:

Buttermilk Brownies

These never-fail, cakelike brownies are a perennial favorite. They're easy to make, rich in chocolate flavor, and always sure to please.

Prep: 30 minutes   **Bake:** 25 minutes   **Oven:** 350°   **Makes:** 24

2   cups all-purpose flour
2   cups granulated sugar
1   teaspoon baking soda
¼   teaspoon salt
1   cup butter
1   cup water
⅓   cup unsweetened cocoa
      powder
2   eggs
½   cup buttermilk
1½   teaspoons vanilla
1   recipe Chocolate-
      Buttermilk Frosting

1 Grease a 15×10×1-inch or a 13×9×2-inch baking pan; set aside. In a medium mixing bowl combine flour, sugar, baking soda, and salt; set aside.

2 In a medium saucepan combine butter, water, and cocoa powder. Bring mixture just to boiling, stirring constantly. Remove from heat. Add the chocolate mixture to the flour mixture; beat with an electric mixer on medium speed until combined. Add the eggs, buttermilk, and vanilla. Beat for 1 minute (batter will be thin). Pour batter into prepared pan.

3 Bake in a 350° oven about 25 minutes for the 15×10×1-inch pan, 35 minutes for the 13×9×2-inch pan, or until a wooden toothpick inserted in the center comes out clean.

4 Pour warm Chocolate-Buttermilk Frosting over the warm brownies, spreading evenly. Cool in pan on a wire rack. Cut into bars.

Chocolate-Buttermilk Frosting: In a medium saucepan combine ¼ cup butter, 3 tablespoons unsweetened cocoa powder, and 3 tablespoons buttermilk. Bring mixture to boiling. Remove from heat. Add 2¼ cups sifted powdered sugar and ½ teaspoon vanilla. Beat until smooth. If desired, stir in ¾ cup coarsely chopped pecans.

Nutrition Facts per brownie: 237 cal., 10 g total fat (6 g sat. fat), 44 mg chol., 185 mg sodium, 35 g carbo., 0 g fiber, 2 g pro.

Cinnamon-Buttermilk Brownies: Prepare brownies as directed, except add 1 teaspoon ground cinnamon to the flour mixture.

To Make Ahead: Prepare and bake brownies as directed; cool completely. Do not frost. Place in a freezer container or bag and freeze for up to 3 months. Before serving, thaw several hours at room temperature. Frost as directed.

Trilevel Brownies

Three sweet layers—a chewy oatmeal cookie crust, a fudgy brownie, and a creamy frosting—stack up to one delectable treat.

Prep: 30 minutes **Bake:** 35 minutes **Oven:** 350° **Makes:** 32

Bottom Layer

- 1 cup quick-cooking rolled oats
- ½ cup all-purpose flour
- ½ cup packed brown sugar
- ¼ teaspoon baking soda
- ½ cup butter, melted

Middle Layer

- 1 egg
- ¾ cup granulated sugar
- ⅔ cup all-purpose flour
- ¼ cup milk
- ¼ cup butter, melted
- 1 ounce unsweetened chocolate, melted and cooled
- 1 teaspoon vanilla
- ¼ teaspoon baking powder
- ½ cup chopped walnuts

Top Layer

- 1 ounce unsweetened chocolate
- 2 tablespoons butter
- 1½ cups sifted powdered sugar
- ½ teaspoon vanilla
  Walnut halves (optional)

1 For the bottom layer, stir together oats, the ½ cup flour, the brown sugar, and baking soda. Stir in the ½ cup melted butter. Pat the mixture into the bottom of an ungreased 11×7×1½-inch baking pan. Bake in a 350° oven for 10 minutes.

2 Meanwhile, for the middle layer, stir together egg, granulated sugar, the ⅔ cup flour, the milk, the ¼ cup melted butter, the 1 ounce melted chocolate, the 1 teaspoon vanilla, and the baking powder until smooth. Fold in chopped walnuts. Spread batter evenly over baked layer in pan. Bake about 25 minutes more or until a wooden toothpick inserted in center comes out clean. Place on a wire rack while preparing top layer.

3 For the top layer, in a medium saucepan heat and stir the 1 ounce chocolate and the 2 tablespoons butter until melted. Stir in the powdered sugar and the ½ teaspoon vanilla. Stir in enough hot water (1 to 2 tablespoons) to make a mixture that is almost pourable. Spread over brownies. If desired, garnish with walnut halves. Cool in pan on wire rack. Cut into bars.

Nutrition Facts per brownie: 141 cal., 7 g total fat (2 g sat. fat), 7 mg chol., 76 mg sodium, 18 g carbo., 1 g fiber, 2 g pro.

Candy Bar Brownies

For a touch of whimsy, serve these bite-size chocolate and peanut butter brownies in paper candy cups. If you prefer a full-size brownie, cut them into 24 squares.

Prep: 25 minutes **Bake:** 25 minutes **Oven:** 350° **Makes:** 70

Crust
1¼ cups finely crushed
        graham crackers (about
        18 graham crackers)
¼ cup granulated sugar
¼ cup finely chopped dry-
        roasted peanuts
½ cup butter, melted

Filling
½ cup butter
2 ounces unsweetened
        chocolate, cut up
1 cup granulated sugar
2 eggs
1 teaspoon vanilla
⅔ cup all-purpose flour
½ cup peanut butter-flavored
        pieces

Topping
1 recipe Peanut Butter
        Frosting
¼ cup peanut halves

1 For crust, in a medium mixing bowl combine crushed graham crackers, the ¼ cup sugar, and the ¼ cup finely chopped peanuts. Stir in ½ cup melted butter. Press mixture evenly into the bottom of an ungreased 11×7×1½-inch baking pan. Bake in a 350° oven for 5 minutes; cool.

2 For filling, in a heavy large saucepan melt the remaining ½ cup butter and chocolate over low heat, stirring occasionally. Remove from heat; stir in the 1 cup sugar, eggs, and vanilla. Stir just until combined. Stir in flour and peanut butter-flavored pieces. Spread evenly over crust.

3 Bake for 20 minutes more. Cool completely in pan on a wire rack. Spread with Peanut Butter Frosting. Cut into 1-inch squares. Place a peanut half on each square.

Peanut Butter Frosting: In a medium mixing bowl beat ¼ cup butter and 2 tablespoons peanut butter with an electric mixer on low speed for 30 seconds. Gradually add 1 cup sifted powdered sugar, beating well. Beat in 1 tablespoon milk and ½ teaspoon vanilla. Gradually beat in 1 cup additional sifted powdered sugar and enough milk to make frosting of spreading consistency.

Nutrition Facts per brownie: 83 cal., 5 g total fat (3 g sat. fat), 15 mg chol., 53 mg sodium, 10 g carbo., 0 g fiber, 1 g pro.

Orange-Glazed Brownies

Irresistibly orange and wonderfully chocolate, these oversize brownies make an indulgent dessert for any dinner from country casual to black-tie elegant.

Prep: 20 minutes **Bake:** 30 minutes **Oven:** 350° **Makes:** 9

4 ounces unsweetened chocolate, chopped
½ cup butter
1 cup granulated sugar
2 eggs
2 teaspoons finely shredded orange peel
1 teaspoon vanilla
¾ cup all-purpose flour
½ cup coarsely chopped walnuts or pecans
1 recipe Chocolate-Orange Glaze

1 In a medium saucepan combine chocolate and butter; heat and stir over low heat until melted. Remove from heat. Stir in sugar, eggs, orange peel, and vanilla. Using a wooden spoon, lightly beat mixture just until combined. Stir in flour and nuts.

2 Spread batter in an ungreased 8×8×2-inch baking pan. Bake in a 350° oven for 30 minutes. Cool completely in pan on a wire rack. Pour Chocolate-Orange Glaze over the cooled brownies, spreading to glaze the top evenly. Let brownies stand at room temperature until glaze is set. Cut into squares.

Chocolate-Orange Glaze: In a heavy small saucepan bring ⅓ cup whipping cream to a gentle boil over medium-low heat, stirring constantly. Remove from heat. Add 3 ounces finely chopped semisweet chocolate and 1 teaspoon finely shredded orange peel. Let stand for 1 minute. Using a wooden spoon, stir mixture until chocolate is melted. Cool glaze for 5 minutes before using.

Nutrition Facts per brownie: 413 cal., 29 g total fat (10 g sat. fat), 73 mg chol., 113 mg sodium, 41 g carbo., 2 g fiber, 6 g pro.

To Make Ahead: Prepare as directed, except line the baking pan with foil, extending foil over the edges of the pan. Grease the foil instead of the pan. Continue as directed; bake and cool completely. Do not frost. Using the edges of the foil, lift the uncut brownies out of the pan and place in a freezer container or bag; freeze up to 3 months. Before serving, thaw for 1 hour. Frost and cut as directed.

Three-Way Fudge Brownies

Baker's choice! The basic recipe produces a rich, fudgy brownie that transforms easily into two more equally tantalizing variations.

Prep: 15 minutes **Bake:** 30 minutes **Oven:** 350° **Makes:** 16 to 20

½ cup butter
2 ounces unsweetened
       chocolate, cut up
1 cup granulated sugar
2 eggs
1 teaspoon vanilla
⅔ cup all-purpose flour

1 Lightly grease an 8×8×2-inch baking pan; set aside. In a heavy medium saucepan melt butter and chocolate over low heat. Remove from heat. Stir in sugar, eggs, and vanilla. Using a wooden spoon, lightly beat mixture just until combined. Stir in flour. Spread batter in prepared pan.

2 Bake in a 350° oven for 30 minutes. Cool completely in pan on a wire rack. Cut into triangles or squares.

Nutrition Facts per brownie: 146 cal., 9 g total fat (5 g sat. fat), 43 mg chol., 71 mg sodium, 17 g carbo., 1 g fiber, 2 g pro.

Crème de Menthe Fudge Brownies: Prepare brownies as directed, except stir ¼ teaspoon mint extract into batter. Bake and cool as directed. For frosting, in a bowl beat ¼ cup butter until fluffy. Gradually add 1 cup sifted powdered sugar, beating well. Beat in 2 tablespoons green crème de menthe. Gradually beat in about ½ cup additional sifted powdered sugar to make of spreading consistency. Spread frosting over cooled brownies. Melt 1 ounce semisweet chocolate over low heat; drizzle over brownies.

Nutrition Facts per brownie: 227 cal., 12 g total fat (7 g sat. fat), 51 mg chol., 102 mg sodium, 28 g carbo., 1 g fiber, 2 g pro.

Fudge Brownies with Peanut Butter Frosting: Prepare, bake, and cool brownies as directed. For frosting, in a medium mixing bowl beat ¼ cup peanut butter with an electric mixer on low speed until fluffy. Gradually add 1 cup sifted powdered sugar, beating well. Beat in ¼ cup milk and 1 teaspoon vanilla. Gradually beat in about ½ cup additional sifted powdered sugar to make of spreading consistency. Spread frosting over brownies; sprinkle with ¼ cup finely chopped peanuts.

Nutrition Facts per brownie: 223 cal., 12 g total fat (6 g sat. fat), 43 mg chol., 101 mg sodium, 28 g carbo., 1 g fiber, 3 g pro.

Chocolate Revel Bars

These fudgy bars have been a favorite of the Better Homes and Gardens® Test Kitchen Home Economists since they first appeared in 1968.

Prep: 30 minutes **Bake:** 25 minutes **Oven:** 350° **Makes:** 60

  1 cup butter, softened
  2 cups packed brown sugar
  1 teaspoon baking soda
  2 eggs
  2 teaspoons vanilla
2½ cups all-purpose flour
  3 cups quick-cooking rolled oats
1½ cups semisweet chocolate pieces
  1 14-ounce can (1¼ cups) sweetened condensed milk or low-fat sweetened condensed milk
  ½ cup chopped walnuts or pecans
  2 teaspoons vanilla

1 Set aside 2 tablespoons of the butter. In a large mixing bowl beat the remaining butter with an electric mixer on medium to high speed for 30 seconds. Add brown sugar and baking soda. Beat until combined, scraping sides of bowl occasionally. Beat in eggs and 2 teaspoons vanilla until combined. Beat in as much of the flour as you can with the mixer. Using a wooden spoon, stir in any remaining flour. Stir in the oats.

2 For filling, in a medium saucepan combine the reserved 2 tablespoons butter, chocolate pieces, and sweetened condensed milk. Cook over low heat until chocolate melts, stirring occasionally. Remove from heat. Stir in the nuts and 2 teaspoons vanilla.

3 Press two-thirds (about 3⅓ cups) of the oat mixture into the bottom of an ungreased 15×10×1-inch baking pan. Spread filling evenly over the oat mixture. Dot remaining oat mixture on the filling.

4 Bake in a 350° oven about 25 minutes or until top is light brown (chocolate filling will look moist). Cool completely in pan on a wire rack. Cut into bars.

Nutrition Facts per bar: 148 cal., 6 g total fat (2 g sat. fat), 17 mg chol., 79 mg sodium, 21 g carbo., 1 g fiber, 3 g pro.

To Make Ahead: Bake the bars as directed; cool completely. Place cut bars in a freezer container or bag and freeze for up to 1 month. Thaw, covered, in the refrigerator about 24 hours.

Chocolate and Peanut Butter Bars

With a chewy oat crust, a creamy peanut butter filling, and a chocolate chip-crumb topping, these delectable bars are a sure winner with both children and adults.

Prep: 20 minutes **Bake:** 27 to 30 minutes **Oven:** 350° **Makes:** 48

Crumb Mixture
- 2 cups quick-cooking rolled oats
- 1¾ cups packed brown sugar
- 1 cup all-purpose flour
- ½ cup whole wheat flour
- 1 teaspoon baking powder
- ½ teaspoon baking soda
- 1 cup butter
- ½ cup chopped peanuts

Topping
- 1 12-ounce package (2 cups) semisweet chocolate pieces

Crust
- 1 egg, beaten

Filling
- 1 14-ounce can (1¼ cups) sweetened condensed milk or low-fat sweetened condensed milk
- ⅓ cup creamy peanut butter

1 For crumb mixture, in a large mixing bowl combine oats, brown sugar, all-purpose flour, whole wheat flour, baking powder, and baking soda. Using a pastry blender, cut in the butter until mixture resembles fine crumbs. Stir in peanuts.

2 For topping, combine 1¾ cups of the crumb mixture and the chocolate pieces; set aside.

3 For crust, stir the egg into the remaining crumb mixture. Press into bottom of an ungreased 15×10×1-inch baking pan. Bake in a 350° oven for 15 minutes.

4 For filling, stir together the sweetened condensed milk and peanut butter until smooth. Pour filling evenly over partially baked crust. Sprinkle topping evenly over filling.

5 Bake 12 to 15 minutes more or until light brown around the edges. Cool completely in pan on a wire rack. Cut into bars.

Nutrition Facts per bar: 163 cal., 9 g total fat (3 g sat. fat), 17 mg chol., 82 mg sodium, 21 g carbo., 1 g fiber, 3 g pro.

To Make Ahead: Bake the bars as directed; cool completely. Place cut bars in a freezer container or bag and freeze for up to 1 month. Thaw, covered, in the refrigerator about 24 hours.

Chocolate Malt Bars

Malted milk balls lend a mild chocolate flavor to these fudge-topped bars. Remember the quick and easy frosting to top other bar cookies and snack cakes.

Prep: 25 minutes   **Bake:** 25 minutes   **Cool:** 2 hours   **Oven:** 350°   **Makes:** 16

⅓ cup butter, softened
½ cup granulated sugar
1 egg
½ cup chocolate-flavored instant malted milk powder
¼ cup milk
1 teaspoon baking powder
1 teaspoon vanilla
1¼ cups all-purpose flour
1 cup malted milk balls, coarsely chopped
1 recipe Quick Fudge Frosting

1 Lightly grease a 9×9×2-inch baking pan; set aside. In a large mixing bowl beat butter and sugar with an electric mixer on medium speed until combined. Add egg, malted milk powder, milk, baking powder, and vanilla. Beat about 2 minutes more or until combined.

2 With mixer on low speed, gradually add flour to the sugar mixture, beating just until combined. Fold in the 1 cup malted milk balls. Spread batter in the prepared pan.

3 Bake in a 350° oven about 25 minutes or until a wooden toothpick inserted near the center comes out clean. Cool completely in pan on a wire rack. Frost cooled bars with Quick Fudge Frosting.

Quick Fudge Frosting: In a medium mixing bowl combine 2½ cups sifted powdered sugar, ¼ cup unsweetened cocoa powder, and 2 tablespoons chocolate-flavored instant malted milk powder. Add ¼ cup softened butter, 3 tablespoons boiling water, and ½ teaspoon vanilla. Beat with an electric mixer on low speed until combined. Beat 1 minute on medium speed. Cool for 20 to 30 minutes or until spreadable.

Nutrition Facts per bar: 259 cal., 9 g total fat (4 g sat. fat), 32 mg chol., 131 mg sodium, 44 g carbo., 0 g fiber, 3 g pro.

To Make Ahead: Prepare bars as directed, except line the pan with foil, extending foil over the edges of the pan. Grease the foil instead of the pan. Continue as directed; bake and cool completely. Do not frost. Using the edges of the foil, lift the uncut brownies out of the pan and place in a freezer container or bag and freeze up to 3 months. Before serving, thaw for 1 hour. Frost and cut as directed.

Chocolate-Caramel Bars

These rich bars feature all kinds of goodies—pecans, coconut, caramels, and milk chocolate—piled on a buttery shortbread crust. And if you prefer, leave out the coconut.

Prep: 20 minutes   **Bake:** 40 to 45 minutes   **Stand:** 10 minutes   **Oven:** 350°   **Makes:** 48

Crust
- 1 cup all-purpose flour
- ½ cup packed brown sugar
- ½ cup butter

Filling
- 1 14-ounce can (1¼ cups) sweetened condensed milk
- 2 teaspoons vanilla
- 2 cups coarsely chopped pecans
- 1 cup flaked coconut

Topping
(handwritten: 1 bag 5.5 oz Werther's)
- 20 vanilla caramels
- 2 tablespoons milk
- 1 cup milk chocolate pieces or semisweet chocolate pieces

1 For crust, in a medium mixing bowl stir together the flour and brown sugar. Using a pastry blender, cut in the butter until the mixture resembles coarse crumbs.

2 Press crumb mixture into the bottom of an ungreased 13×9×2-inch baking pan. Bake in a 350° oven for 15 minutes.

3 Meanwhile, for filling, combine sweetened condensed milk and vanilla. Sprinkle pecans and coconut over partially baked crust. Pour filling over pecans and coconut.

4 Bake for 25 to 30 minutes more or until the filling is set. Cool in pan on a wire rack for 10 minutes.

5 In a small saucepan combine caramels and milk. Cook and stir over medium-low heat just until caramels are melted. Drizzle caramel mixture over filling. Sprinkle with chocolate pieces. Cool completely. Cut into bars.

Nutrition Facts per bar: 132 cal., 8 g total fat (2 g sat. fat), 6 mg chol., 42 mg sodium, 15 g carbo., 1 g fiber, 2 g pro.

Blondies

Searching for simplicity in a bar? Here it is. Mix these delightful butterscotch treats in the same saucepan you use to melt the butter.

Prep: 25 minutes   **Bake:** 25 minutes   **Oven:** 350°   **Makes:** 36

2   cups packed brown sugar
⅔   cup butter
2   eggs
2   teaspoons vanilla
2   cups all-purpose flour
1   teaspoon baking powder
¼   teaspoon baking soda
1   cup (6 ounces) semisweet chocolate pieces
1   cup chopped nuts

1 Lightly grease a 13×9×2-inch baking pan; set aside. In a medium saucepan heat brown sugar and butter over medium heat until sugar dissolves, stirring constantly. Cool slightly. Using a wooden spoon, stir in eggs, one at a time, and vanilla. Stir in flour, baking powder, and baking soda. Spread batter in the prepared pan. Sprinkle with chocolate and nuts.

2 Bake in a 350° oven for 25 minutes. Cool slightly in pan on a wire rack. Cut into bars while warm; cool completely in pan.

Nutrition Facts per bar: 138 cal., 7 g total fat (2 g sat. fat), 21 mg chol., 61 mg sodium, 18 g carbo., 0 g fiber, 2 g pro.

To Make Ahead: Bake the bars as directed; cool completely. Place cut bars in a freezer container or bag and freeze for up to 1 month. Thaw, covered, in the refrigerator about 24 hours.

tied with a bow

Looking for a small token to thank someone for services rendered? Or, maybe small gifts to pass around the office? Bake a batch of rich, luscious bar cookies or brownies and cut into squares, triangles, or diamonds (see tip, page 34). You may want to cut them into more generous portions than directed in the recipe. Wrap the bars individually in plastic wrap and tie with fabric ribbon. If you like, attach a small pin or ornament to the ribbon to personalize the gift.

Pecan Pie Bars

These scrumptious bars boast a pecan pie filling baked over a buttery shortbread crust.

Prep: 20 minutes   **Bake:** 40 to 45 minutes   **Oven:** 375°   **Makes:** 24

Crust
- 1¼ cups all-purpose flour
- 3 tablespoons brown sugar
- ½ cup butter

Filling
- 2 eggs
- ½ cup packed brown sugar
- ¾ cup chopped pecans
- ½ cup light corn syrup
- 2 tablespoons butter, melted
- 1 teaspoon vanilla

1 For crust, combine flour and the 3 tablespoons brown sugar. Cut in the ½ cup butter until mixture resembles coarse crumbs. Pat crumb mixture into an ungreased 11×7×1½-inch baking pan. Bake in 375° oven for 20 minutes.

2 Meanwhile, for filling, beat eggs with fork. Stir in the ½ cup brown sugar, pecans, corn syrup, melted butter, and vanilla. Pour over the baked crust, spreading evenly.

3 Bake for 20 to 25 minutes more or until filling is set. Cool completely in pan on a wire rack. Cut into bars. Store bars in the refrigerator.

Nutrition Facts per bar: 136 cal., 8 g total fat (3 g sat. fat), 31 mg chol., 67 mg sodium, 16 g carbo., 0 g fiber, 1 g pro.

To Make Ahead: Bake the bars as directed; cool completely. Place cut bars in a freezer container or bag and freeze for up to 1 month. Thaw, covered, in the refrigerator about 24 hours.

a new look for bar cookies

Forget squares and rectangles. To give brownies and bars a new look, I cut them into triangles and diamonds instead of the traditional squares and rectangles.

To make triangles, cut bars into 2- or 2½-inch squares. Cut each square in half diagonally. Or, cut bars into rectangles and cut each diagonally into triangles.

To make diamonds, first cut parallel lines 1 or 1½ inches apart down the length of the pan. Then cut diagonal lines the same distance apart across the pan, forming diamond shapes.

Jan Miller

Test Kitchen Home Economist

Toasted Hazelnut Bars

Toasting the hazelnuts enriches their flavor as well as aids in removing the skins. To remove the skins, place the warm nuts on a clean kitchen towel and rub vigorously until the skins come off.

Prep: 20 minutes   **Bake:** 50 minutes   **Oven:** 350°   **Makes:** 48

Crust
- ½ cup butter, softened
- 2 3-ounce packages cream cheese, softened
- ½ cup packed brown sugar
- 2 cups all-purpose flour

Filling
- 2 cups granulated sugar
- 1½ cups buttermilk
- 4 eggs
- ½ cup butter, melted
- ⅓ cup all-purpose flour
- 2 teaspoons vanilla
- ½ teaspoon salt
- 2 cups toasted chopped hazelnuts (filberts)

Topping
- Sifted powdered sugar

1 For crust, in a large mixing bowl beat the ½ cup softened butter, cream cheese, brown sugar, and the 2 cups flour with an electric mixer on medium to high speed until well combined. With lightly floured hands pat mixture onto the bottom and up sides of an ungreased 15×10×1-inch baking pan. Bake in a 350° oven for 15 minutes.

2 Meanwhile, for filling, in a medium mixing bowl beat together granulated sugar, buttermilk, eggs, the ½ cup melted butter, the ⅓ cup flour, vanilla, and salt with an electric mixer on low speed until combined. Stir in nuts. Pour into crust.

3 Bake in a 350° oven for 35 minutes or until golden. Cool completely in pan on a wire rack. Cut into bars. Sprinkle with powdered sugar. Store bars in the refrigerator.

Nutrition Facts per bar: 146 cal., 9 g total fat (4 g sat. fat), 32 mg chol., 75 mg sodium, 16 g carbo., 1 g fiber, 2 g pro.

Double-Cherry Streusel Bars

The season for fresh cherries is brief, but with this very cherry bar you can enjoy them any time of the year—thanks to dried tart cherries and cherry preserves.

Prep: 20 minutes **Bake:** 32 to 37 minutes **Oven:** 350° **Makes:** 48

2 cups water
1 cup dried tart cherries or dried cranberries, snipped

Crust

2 cups quick-cooking rolled oats
1½ cups all-purpose flour
1½ cups packed brown sugar
1 teaspoon baking powder
½ teaspoon baking soda
1 cup butter
½ cup coarsely chopped slivered almonds

Filling

2 12-ounce jars cherry preserves
1 teaspoon finely shredded lemon peel

Drizzle

½ cup semisweet chocolate pieces
1 teaspoon shortening, melted

1 In a small saucepan bring water to boiling. Remove from heat. Add dried cherries or cranberries and let stand for 10 minutes or until softened. Drain and set aside.

2 For crust, in a large mixing bowl combine oats, flour, brown sugar, baking powder, and baking soda. Using a pastry blender, cut in the butter until the mixture resembles coarse crumbs. Reserve 1 cup of the crumb mixture. Stir the almonds into the reserved crumb mixture; set aside.

3 Press remaining crumb mixture into the bottom of an ungreased 15×10×1-inch baking pan. Bake in a 350° oven for 12 minutes.

4 Meanwhile, for filling, stir together the drained cherries, cherry preserves, and lemon peel. Spread the filling evenly over baked crust; sprinkle with reserved crumb mixture.

5 Bake for 20 to 25 minutes more or until top is golden brown. Cool completely in pan on a wire rack. In a small saucepan combine the chocolate pieces and shortening; heat over medium-low heat until chocolate is melted. Drizzle melted chocolate mixture over baked bars. Cut into bars.

Nutrition Facts per bar: 144 cal., 5 g total fat (2 g sat. fat), 10 mg chol., 63 mg sodium, 24 g carbo., 1 g fiber, 1 g pro.

To Make Ahead: Prepare bars as directed, except line the pan with foil, extending foil over the edges of the pan. Grease the foil instead of the pan. Continue as directed; bake and cool completely. Do not drizzle with chocolate. Using the edges of the foil, lift the uncut bars out of the pan and place in a freezer container or bag and freeze up to 3 months. Before serving, thaw for 1 hour. Drizzle with chocolate and cut as directed.

Orange-Coconut Bars

Brighten a dreary day with a batch of these zingy bars. Use fresh-squeezed orange juice for optimal flavor.

Prep: 20 minutes   **Bake:** 38 to 40 minutes   **Oven:** 350°   **Makes:** 16

Crust
- ½ cup all-purpose flour
- ¼ cup granulated sugar
- ¼ cup butter
- ½ cup finely chopped pecans

Filling
- 2 eggs
- ¾ cup granulated sugar
- 2 tablespoons all-purpose flour
- 1½ teaspoons finely shredded orange peel
- 3 tablespoons orange juice
- ¼ teaspoon baking powder
- 1 cup coconut

1 For crust, in a medium mixing bowl combine the ½ cup flour and the ¼ cup sugar. Using a pastry blender, cut in butter until mixture resembles coarse crumbs. Stir in pecans. Press mixture into the bottom of an ungreased 8×8×2-inch baking pan. Bake in a 350° oven for 18 to 20 minutes or until golden.

2 Meanwhile, for filling, in another medium mixing bowl combine eggs, the ¾ cup sugar, the 2 tablespoons flour, orange peel, orange juice, and baking powder. Beat for 2 minutes with an electric mixer or until combined. Stir in coconut. Pour coconut mixture over baked crust.

3 Bake 20 minutes more or until edges are light brown and center is set. Cool completely in pan on a wire rack. Cut into bars. Store bars in the refrigerator.

Nutrition Facts per bar: 144 cal., 8 g total fat (4 g sat. fat), 35 mg chol., 46 mg sodium, 18 g carbo., 1 g fiber, 2 g pro.

Lemon Bars Deluxe

Company coming? This recipe makes a big batch of these classic tangy treats. Before serving, top with an additional dusting of powdered sugar.

Prep: 20 minutes   **Bake:** 45 to 50 minutes   **Oven:** 350°   **Makes:** 30

Crust
2 cups all-purpose flour
½ cup sifted powdered sugar
1 cup butter

Filling
4 beaten eggs
1½ cups granulated sugar
1 to 2 teaspoons finely
   shredded lemon peel
   (set aside)
⅓ cup lemon juice
¼ cup all-purpose flour
½ teaspoon baking powder

Topping
Powdered sugar (optional)

1 For crust, in a medium mixing bowl stir together the 2 cups flour and the ½ cup powdered sugar. Using a pastry blender, cut in the butter until mixture clings together. Press into the bottom of an ungreased 13×9×2-inch baking pan. Bake crust in a 350° oven for 20 to 25 minutes or until light brown.

2 For filling, in a bowl beat together eggs, granulated sugar, and lemon juice. Combine the ¼ cup flour and baking powder; stir into the egg mixture. Stir in lemon peel. Pour over crust.

3 Bake in a 350° oven 25 minutes more. Cool completely in pan on a wire rack. Cut into bars. If desired, sift additional powdered sugar over cooled bars. Store bars in the refrigerator.

Nutrition Facts per bar: 141 cal., 7 g total fat (4 g sat. fat), 45 mg chol., 77 mg sodium, 19 g carbo., 0 g fiber, 2 g pro.

To Make Ahead: Bake the bars as directed; cool completely. Place cut bars in a freezer container or bag and freeze for up to 1 month. Thaw, covered, in the refrigerator about 24 hours.

a shred of peel

I love the burst of flavor citrus peel gives to cookies. The little time it takes to shred fresh peel is worth the effort.

If a recipe calls for shredded lime, orange, or lemon peel, use only the colored surface of the peel, not the bitter tasting, spongy, white pith. Hand-graters and zesters are convenient, but you can also use a vegetable peeler to remove thin layers of peel. Finely mince the peel with a sharp kitchen knife. Prepare extra peel to keep on hand, and freeze it in a resealable plastic freezer bag.

Jill Moberly

Test Kitchen Home Economist

Blueberry Bars

You can enjoy these luscious crumb-topped fruit bars year-round because they're made with frozen blueberries and preserves.

Prep: 20 minutes **Bake:** 55 minutes **Oven:** 350° **Makes:** 25

Crust
1½ cups quick-cooking rolled
       oats
 1 cup all-purpose flour
 ¾ cup packed brown sugar
 ¾ cup butter

Filling
 1 cup frozen blueberries
 ½ cup blueberry, raspberry,
       or strawberry preserves
 1 teaspoon finely shredded
       lemon peel

1 Line an 8×8×2-inch baking pan with foil; set aside. In a medium bowl combine oats, flour, and brown sugar. Cut in butter until pieces are the size of small peas. Reserve 1 cup of the mixture. Press remaining oat mixture into the bottom of prepared pan. Bake in a 350° oven for 25 minutes.

2 For filling, in bowl combine frozen blueberries, preserves, and lemon peel. Carefully spread over baked crust. Sprinkle with reserved oat mixture, pressing lightly into blueberry mixture.

3 Bake about 30 minutes more or until top is golden. Cool completely in pan on a wire rack. Cut into bars.

Nutrition Facts per bar: 135 cal., 6 g total fat (4 g sat. fat), 16 mg chol., 65 mg sodium, 19 g carbo., 1 g fiber, 1 g pro.

To Make Ahead: Bake the bars as directed; cool completely. Place cut bars in a freezer container or bag and freeze for up to 1 month. Thaw, covered, in the refrigerator about 24 hours.

spice and everything nice

Freshness counts, even with spices. And, since you use just a speck of spice at a time, it's easy to lose track of when you purchased any individual spice. The flavor in spices comes from volatile oils that lose their punch over time. Follow these tips to ensure the ultimate flavor from your spices.

• Keep all spices in well-sealed air-tight containers.

• Store spices in a cool, dry place. Write the date of purchase on the container.

• Buy spices in small amounts, and throw away any spices older than 6 months.

• For the freshest flavor, buy whole spices and grind them just before using.

Danish Pastry Apple Bars

If your family loves apple pie (and whose doesn't?), these bars will be a sure winner at dessert time. The perfect pastry—so tender and so flaky—tops off the perfectly spiced apple filling.

Prep: 30 minutes   **Bake:** 50 minutes   **Oven:** 375°   **Makes:** 32

Pastry
2½ cups all-purpose flour
1 teaspoon salt
1 cup shortening
1 egg yolk
  Milk

Filling
1 cup corn flakes
8 to 10 tart baking apples, such as Cortland, Rome, Beauty, or Granny Smith, peeled and sliced (8 cups)
½ cup granulated sugar
1 teaspoon ground cinnamon
1 egg white
1 tablespoon water

Topping
  Sifted powdered sugar or whipped cream (optional)

1 For pastry, in a large mixing bowl stir together the flour and salt. Using a pastry blender, cut in shortening until mixture resembles coarse crumbs. Lightly beat egg yolk in a glass measuring cup. Add enough milk to egg yolk to make ⅔ cup liquid total; mix well. Stir egg yolk mixture into flour mixture; mix well. Divide dough in half.

2 On a lightly floured surface, roll half of the dough to an 18×12-inch rectangle; fit into and up the sides of a 15×10×1-inch baking pan. Sprinkle with corn flakes; top with apples. Combine sugar and cinnamon; sprinkle over apples. Roll the remaining dough to a 16×12-inch rectangle; place over apples. Seal edges; cut slits in top for steam to escape. Beat egg white and water; brush over pastry.

3 Bake in a 375° oven about 50 minutes or until golden. Cool in pan on a wire rack. Serve warm or cool. If desired, top with powdered sugar or whipped cream.

Nutrition Facts per bar: 128 cal., 7 g total fat (2 g sat. fat), 7 mg chol., 80 mg sodium, 16 g carbo., 1 g fiber, 1 g pro.

Spiced Pumpkin Bars

One of these moist, cakelike bars and a tall glass of apple cider makes a satisfying snack, especially on a crisp autumn afternoon.

Prep: 15 minutes   **Bake:** 25 to 30 minutes   **Oven:** 350°   **Makes:** 24

  2 cups all-purpose flour
  2 teaspoons baking powder
  2 teaspoons ground
       cinnamon
  1 teaspoon baking soda
  ¼ teaspoon salt
  4 eggs
  1 15-ounce can pumpkin
1⅔ cups granulated sugar
  1 cup cooking oil
  ¾ cup chopped pecans
       (optional)
  1 recipe Cream Cheese
       Frosting
       Pecan halves (optional)

1 In a medium bowl stir together flour, baking powder, cinnamon, baking soda, and salt; set aside.

2 In a large mixing bowl beat together eggs, pumpkin, sugar, and oil with an electric mixer on medium speed. Add the flour mixture; beat until well combined. If desired, stir in chopped pecans. Spread batter into an ungreased 15×10×1-inch baking pan.

3 Bake in a 350° oven for 25 to 30 minutes or until a wooden toothpick inserted in the center comes out clean. Cool completely in pan on a wire rack. Frost with Cream Cheese Frosting. If desired, top with additional pecan halves. Cut into squares. Store in the refrigerator.

Cream Cheese Frosting: In a medium mixing bowl beat together one 3-ounce package cream cheese, softened; ¼ cup butter, softened; and 1 teaspoon vanilla until fluffy. Gradually add 2 cups sifted powdered sugar, beating until smooth.

Nutrition Facts per bar: 250 cal., 13 g total fat (4 g sat. fat), 45 mg chol., 147 mg sodium, 31 g carbo., 1 g fiber, 3 g pro.

Banana Bars

A splash of brandy in the buttery frosting lends a sophisticated allure to these toffee-flecked bars. If you're baking them with kids in mind, use the milk instead of the brandy for a homespun treat.

Prep: 20 minutes   **Bake:** 25 minutes   **Oven:** 350°   **Makes:** 48

½ cup butter, softened
1⅓ cups granulated sugar
1½ teaspoons baking powder
½ teaspoon baking soda
¼ teaspoon salt
1 egg
1 cup mashed bananas
      (about 3 medium)
½ cup dairy sour cream
1 teaspoon vanilla
2 cups all-purpose flour
¾ cup chocolate-covered
      toffee pieces or almond
      brickle pieces
¾ cup toasted chopped
      almonds (optional)
1 recipe Brandied Brown
      Butter Frosting

1 Lightly grease a 15×10×1-inch baking pan; set aside. In a large mixing bowl beat butter with an electric mixer on medium to high speed for 30 seconds. Add sugar, baking powder, baking soda, and salt; beat until combined, scraping sides of bowl occasionally. Beat in the egg, mashed bananas, sour cream, and vanilla until combined. Beat or stir in the flour. Stir in toffee pieces and, if desired, almonds. Pour the batter into the prepared baking pan, spreading evenly.

2 Bake in a 350° oven about 25 minutes or until a wooden toothpick inserted near the center comes out clean. Cool completely in pan on a wire rack. Spread with Brandied Brown Butter Frosting. Cut into bars.

Brandied Browned Butter Frosting: In a small saucepan heat ⅓ cup butter over low heat until melted. Continue heating until the butter turns light brown. Remove from heat; pour into a medium mixing bowl. Add 2½ cups sifted powdered sugar, 1 tablespoon brandy or milk, and 1 teaspoon vanilla. Beat with an electric mixer on low speed until combined. Beat on high to medium speed, adding enough milk to make frosting of spreading consistency. Use immediately.

Nutrition Facts per bar: 115 cal., 5 g total fat (1 g sat. fat), 10 mg chol., 77 mg sodium, 18 g carbo., 0 g fiber, 1 g pro.

To Make Ahead: Prepare and bake bars as directed; cool completely. Do not frost. Place in a freezer container or bag and freeze for up to 3 months. Before serving, thaw several hours at room temperature. Frost as directed.

Strawberry Cheesecake Bars

These bars boast a little bit of everything—a buttery crust, a cheesecake filling topped with strawberry preserves, and an almond-crumb topping.

Prep: 30 minutes   **Bake:** 42 to 45 minutes   **Chill:** 3 hours   **Oven:** 350°   **Makes:** 32

Crust
- 1¼ cups all-purpose flour
- ½ cup packed brown sugar
- ½ cup finely chopped sliced almonds
- ½ cup butter-flavor shortening or shortening

Filling
- 2 8-ounce packages cream cheese, softened
- ⅔ cup granulated sugar
- 2 eggs
- ¾ teaspoon almond extract

Topping
- 1 cup seedless strawberry or raspberry preserves
- ½ cup flaked coconut
- ½ cup sliced almonds

1 In a medium mixing bowl combine flour, brown sugar, and finely chopped almonds. Using a pastry blender, cut in shortening until mixture resembles fine crumbs. Set aside ½ cup of the crumb mixture for topping.

2 For crust, press the remaining crumb mixture into the bottom of an ungreased 13×9×2-inch baking pan. Bake in a 350° oven for 12 to 15 minutes or until the edges are golden.

3 Meanwhile, for filling, in another medium mixing bowl beat cream cheese, granulated sugar, eggs, and almond extract with an electric mixer on medium speed until smooth. Spread over hot crust. Bake for 15 minutes more.

4 Stir preserves; spread over cream cheese mixture. In a small bowl combine reserved crumb mixture, coconut, and almonds. Sprinkle over preserves.

5 Return to oven; bake 15 minutes more. Cool completely in pan on a wire rack. Chill about 3 hours before cutting into bars. Store bars in the refrigerator.

Nutrition Facts per bar: 184 cal., 11 g total fat (4 g sat. fat), 29 mg chol., 52 mg sodium, 19 g carbo., 1 g fiber, 3 g pro.

To Make Ahead: Bake the bars as directed; cool completely. Place cut bars in a freezer container or bag and freeze for up to 1 month. Thaw, covered, in the refrigerator about 24 hours.

Sliced Cookies

Butterfly Cookies

Cheesecake Cookies

Soft-style cream cheese makes a ready-to-spread frosting for these tender wafers. Frost just enough cookies to eat at one time. Save the remaining cookies and cream cheese for another day.

Prep: 20 minutes   **Bake:** 8 to 10 minutes   **Chill:** 4 to 48 hours   **Oven:** 375°   **Makes:** 48

¾ cup butter, softened
1 3-ounce package cream cheese, softened
½ cup granulated sugar
1 teaspoon vanilla
1½ cups all-purpose flour
1 8-ounce container soft-style cream cheese with strawberries
   Fresh strawberries, halved (optional)

1 In a medium mixing bowl beat butter and plain cream cheese with an electric mixer on medium to high speed for 30 seconds. Add sugar and vanilla; beat until combined, scraping sides of bowl occasionally. Using a wooden spoon, stir in flour.

2 Divide dough in half. Shape each half of dough into a 6-inch-long roll. Wrap rolls in plastic wrap or waxed paper. Chill in the refrigerator for 4 to 48 hours.

3 Using a sharp knife, cut dough into ¼-inch slices. Place slices 2 inches apart on an ungreased cookie sheet.

4 Bake in a 375° oven 8 to 10 minutes or until edges are light brown. Cool on cookie sheet for 1 minute. Transfer to a wire rack; cool completely. Just before serving, spread cookies with strawberry cream cheese. If desired, top with strawberry halves.

Nutrition Facts per cookie: 70 cal., 5 g total fat (3 g sat. fat), 14 mg chol., 51 mg sodium, 6 g carbo., 0 g fiber, 1 g pro.

freeze with ease

Stash a roll of sliced cookie dough in the freezer for unexpected guests or spur-of-the-moment snacks. I can have fresh-baked cookies, ready and waiting, in 30 minutes when I start with a roll of frozen dough.

Shape the rolls as directed in the recipe, wrap in plastic wrap, and freeze until firm. Wrap again in heavy foil or place in freezer bags and freeze for up to one month. When you're ready to bake the cookies, thaw the roll of cookie dough in the refrigerator until you can slice it. For the roundest slices, use a thin, sharp knife to slice the cookies and rotate the roll frequently to avoid flattening one side.

Kay Springer
Test Kitchen Home Economist

Lemon and Poppy Seed Melts

To give these cookies a shimmering glow, add a tablespoon or two of edible glitter to the powdered sugar. If necessary, freshen the sugar coating just before serving.

Prep: 20 minutes   **Bake:** 7 to 9 minutes   **Chill:** 4 to 24 hours   **Oven:** 375°   **Makes:** 36

½ cup butter, softened
½ cup granulated sugar
1 tablespoon poppy seed
⅛ teaspoon baking soda
1 egg yolk
1 tablespoon milk
2 teaspoons finely shredded
     lemon peel
½ teaspoon vanilla
1½ cups all-purpose flour
1 cup sifted powdered sugar
     Yellow edible glitter
        (optional)

1 In a medium mixing bowl beat butter with an electric mixer on medium to high speed for 30 seconds. Add granulated sugar, poppy seed, and baking soda; beat until combined, scraping sides of bowl occasionally. Beat in egg yolk, milk, lemon peel, and vanilla until combined. Beat in as much flour as you can with the mixer. Using a wooden spoon, stir in any remaining flour.

2 Divide dough in half. Shape each half into a 9-inch-long roll. Wrap in plastic wrap or waxed paper. Chill in the refrigerator for 4 to 24 hours. Using a sharp knife, cut dough into ½-inch slices. Place slices 1 inch apart on ungreased cookie sheet.

3 Bake in a 375° oven for 7 to 9 minutes or until edges are firm and bottoms are light brown. Place powdered sugar in a plastic bag. If desired, add edible glitter to powdered sugar. While still warm, transfer several at a time to the bag. Gently shake until coated. Transfer cookies to a wire rack; cool. When completely cool, gently shake cookies again in powdered sugar.

Nutrition Facts per cookie: 64 cal., 3 g total fat (2 g sat. fat), 13 mg chol., 31 mg sodium, 9 g carbo., 0 g fiber, 1 g pro.

To Make Ahead: Bake and cool cookies as directed. Do not coat with sugar. Place in freezer container; freeze up to 3 months. Thaw about 15 minutes. Shake in powdered sugar as directed.

Praline Rounds

These crisp, tender cookies celebrate the famous praline duo of brown sugar and pecans. A brown sugar-and-cream frosting drizzled over the tops adds even more southern-style sweetness.

Prep: 20 minutes **Bake:** 8 to 10 minutes **Chill:** 4 to 48 hours **Oven:** 375° **Makes:** 72

½ cup butter, softened
½ cup shortening
1 cup packed brown sugar
½ teaspoon baking powder
¼ teaspoon baking soda
¼ teaspoon salt
1 egg
2 tablespoons milk
1 teaspoon vanilla
3 cups all-purpose flour
1 cup finely chopped pecans
1 recipe Brown Sugar
    Frosting

1 In a large mixing bowl beat butter and shortening with an electric mixer on medium to high speed for 30 seconds. Add brown sugar, baking powder, baking soda, and salt; beat until combined, scraping sides of bowl occasionally. Beat in egg, milk, and vanilla until combined. Beat in as much of the flour as you can with the mixer. Using a wooden spoon, stir in any remaining flour and ½ cup of the pecans.

2 Divide dough in half. Shape each half of dough into a 10-inch-long roll. Wrap rolls in plastic wrap or waxed paper. Chill in the refrigerator for 4 to 48 hours.

3 Using a sharp knife, cut dough into ¼-inch slices. Place slices 2 inches apart on an ungreased cookie sheet.

4 Bake in a 375° oven for 8 to 10 minutes or until edges are firm. Transfer to a wire rack; cool. Sprinkle with remaining pecans. Drizzle with warm Brown Sugar Frosting.

Brown Sugar Frosting: In a small saucepan combine 1 cup packed brown sugar, ¼ cup butter, and ¼ cup light cream. Heat and stir over medium heat until mixture comes to a full boil. Boil for 1 minute, stirring constantly. Remove from heat. Add 1⅓ cups sifted powdered sugar. Beat with a wire whisk or fork until smooth. (Frosting will thicken as it cools. If necessary, add a few drops of water to make of drizzling consistency.)

Nutrition Facts per cookie: 91 cal., 5 g total fat (2 g sat. fat), 9 mg chol., 40 mg sodium, 12 g carbo., 0 g fiber, 1 g pro.

To Make Ahead: Bake and cool cookies as directed, but do not drizzle with frosting. Place in a freezer container or bag and freeze up to 3 months. Thaw cookies about 15 minutes. Prepare frosting and drizzle over thawed cookies.

Two-Tone Biscotti

The toothsome flavors of rich chocolate and delicate orange meet in this cookie—the perfect biscotti to nibble with a steaming cup of espresso.

Prep: 20 minutes **Bake:** 45 to 50 minutes **Stand:** 1 hour **Oven:** 375°/325° **Makes:** 70

⅔ cup butter, softened
1⅓ cups granulated sugar
3 teaspoons baking powder
¼ teaspoon salt
4 eggs
1 teaspoon vanilla
4 cups all-purpose flour
1½ cups semisweet chocolate pieces, melted and cooled
1 cup finely chopped hazelnuts (filberts)
1 tablespoon finely shredded orange peel

1 In a large mixing bowl beat butter with an electric mixer on medium to high speed for 30 seconds. Add sugar, baking powder, and salt; beat until combined, scraping sides of bowl occasionally. Beat in eggs and vanilla until combined. Beat in as much of the flour as you can with the mixer. Using a wooden spoon, stir in any remaining flour.

2 Divide dough in half. Place one half in another bowl. Into half of the dough, stir the melted chocolate and ½ cup of the nuts. Into the other half of the dough, stir the orange peel and the remaining nuts.

3 Divide each half of the dough into 3 portions. With lightly floured hands, shape each portion into a rope about 14 inches long. Place a rope of each color side by side on an ungreased cookie sheet. Twist ropes around each other several times. Flatten slightly to a 2-inch width. Repeat with the remaining ropes, placing twists about 4 inches apart on the cookie sheet.

4 Bake in a 375° oven 25 minutes or until light brown. Cool on cookie sheet for 1 hour or until completely cool.

5 Transfer loaves to a cutting board. Cut each loaf into ½-inch slices. Place slices on the same cookie sheet. Bake in a 325° oven for 10 minutes. Turn slices over and bake for 10 to 15 minutes more or until crisp. Transfer to wire rack; cool.

Nutrition Facts per cookie: 88 cal., 4 g total fat (1 g sat. fat), 14 mg chol., 43 mg sodium, 10 g carbo., 1 g fiber, 1 g pro.

To Make Ahead: Bake cookies as directed; cool completely. Place cookies in a freezer container or bag and freeze up to 3 months. Before serving; thaw 15 minutes.

Lemon-Pistachio Biscotti

Coffeehouses have turned biscotti, the twice-baked Italian cookie, into a household word. If you're a pistachio aficionado, this is the biscotti for you.

Prep: 35 minutes **Bake:** 36 to 43 minutes **Stand:** 30 minutes **Oven:** 375°/325° **Makes:** 36

⅓ cup butter, softened
⅔ cup granulated sugar
2 teaspoons baking powder
½ teaspoon salt
2 eggs
1 teaspoon vanilla
4 teaspoons finely shredded lemon peel
2 cups all-purpose flour
1½ cups unsalted pistachio nuts (6 ounces)
1 recipe Lemon Icing

1 Line an extra-large cookie sheet or 2 cookie sheets with parchment paper or lightly grease; set aside. In a large mixing bowl beat butter with an electric mixer on medium to high speed for 30 seconds. Add sugar, baking powder, and salt; beat until combined, scraping sides of bowl occasionally. Beat in eggs and vanilla until combined. Beat in lemon peel and as much of the flour as you can with the mixer. Using a wooden spoon, stir in any remaining flour and nuts.

2 On a lightly floured surface, divide dough into 3 equal portions. Shape each portion into an 8-inch-long loaf. Flatten loaves to about 2½ inches wide. Place at least 3 inches apart on prepared cookie sheet(s).

3 Bake in a 375° oven for 20 to 25 minutes or until golden brown and tops are cracked. (Loaves will spread slightly.) Cool on cookie sheet for 30 minutes.

4 Transfer loaves to a cutting board. Cut each loaf diagonally into ½-inch slices. Place slices, cut sides down, on the same parchment-lined cookie sheets. Bake in a 325° oven for 8 minutes. Turn slices over and bake 8 to 10 minutes more or until dry and crisp. Transfer to a wire rack; cool. Dip ends into or drizzle with Lemon Icing.

Lemon Icing: In a small mixing bowl stir together 1 cup sifted powdered sugar and 1 teaspoon finely shredded lemon peel. Stir in enough milk or lemon juice (1 to 2 tablespoons) to make icing of drizzling consistency.

Nutrition Facts per cookie: 99 cal., 5 g total fat (1 g sat. fat), 16 mg chol., 71 mg sodium, 13 g carbo., 1 g fiber, 2 g pro.

To Make Ahead: Bake and cool cookies as directed, but do not dip in icing. Place in a freezer container or bag and freeze up to 3 months. Thaw cookies about 15 minutes. Dip cookies into or drizzle with icing.

Molasses Slices

Use either canned frosting or your favorite homemade frosting to stuff these cookie sandwiches. Pair them with a frosty mug of milk for a hearty snack.

Prep: 25 minutes   **Bake:** 8 minutes   **Chill:** 6 to 26 hours   **Oven:** 375°   **Makes:** 54

½ cup butter, softened
½ cup shortening
¾ cup granulated sugar
1½ teaspoons baking soda
½ teaspoon ground
     cinnamon
¼ teaspoon ground nutmeg
¼ teaspoon ground ginger
¼ teaspoon ground cloves
1 egg
½ cup molasses
2¼ cups all-purpose flour
1¼ cups canned vanilla
     frosting

1 In a large mixing bowl beat butter and shortening with an electric mixer on medium to high speed for 30 seconds. Add sugar, baking soda, cinnamon, nutmeg, ginger, and cloves. Beat until combined, scraping the sides of the bowl occasionally. Beat in egg and molasses until combined. Beat in as much of the flour as you can with the mixer. Using a wooden spoon, stir in any remaining flour.

2 Cover and chill dough for 2 hours or until easy to handle. Divide dough in half. Shape each half into a 9-inch-long roll. Wrap rolls in plastic wrap or waxed paper. Chill in the refrigerator for 4 to 24 hours.

3 Using a sharp knife, cut dough into ¼-inch slices. Place slices about 2 inches apart on an ungreased cookie sheet.

4 Bake in a 375° oven about 8 minutes or until edges are firm. Cool on cookie sheet for 2 minutes. Transfer cookies to a wire rack; cool completely. Just before serving, spread the bottoms of half the cookies with frosting; place bottoms of other cookies on top of the frosting.

Nutrition Facts per cookie sandwich: 192 cal., 10 g total fat (4 g sat. fat), 18 mg chol., 124 mg sodium, 26 g carbo., 1 g fiber, 1 g pro.

To Make Ahead: Bake and cool cookies as directed, but do not frost. Place in a freezer container or bag and freeze up to 3 months. Thaw cookies about 15 minutes. Spread frosting over thawed cookies as directed.

Bite-Size Jam Swirls

Cream cheese imparts a tangy taste and delicate texture to the dough while a swirl of jam and a coating of coarse sugar gives a gemlike sparkle to the finished cookies.

Prep: 30 minutes **Bake:** 15 minutes **Chill:** 3 hours **Oven:** 375° **Makes:** 36

3 cups all-purpose flour
  Dash salt
1 8-ounce package cream
    cheese
1 cup butter
½ cup raspberry or
    strawberry jam
1 cup finely chopped
    walnuts
  Coarse sugar

1 In a large mixing bowl combine flour and salt. Using a pastry blender, cut in cream cheese and butter until the mixture resembles fine crumbs and begins to cling together. Form mixture into a ball; knead until smooth. Divide dough in half. Wrap each half in plastic wrap; chill about 1 hour or until easy to handle.

2 On a lightly floured surface, roll half of the dough at a time to ¼-inch thickness. Fold dough into thirds. Wrap in plastic wrap and chill for 2 hours.

3 Roll each half of dough into a 14×12-inch rectangle. Spread each with half of the jam to within ½ inch of edges; sprinkle each with half of the nuts. Starting from one of the long sides, roll up, jelly-roll style; seal edges.

4 Using a sharp knife, cut dough into ½-inch slices. Dip one cut side of each slice in coarse sugar. Place slices, sugar side up, 1 inch apart on an ungreased cookie sheet.

5 Bake in a 375° oven about 15 minutes or until light brown. Transfer cookies to a wire rack; cool.

Nutrition Facts per cookie: 128 cal., 9 g total fat (5 g sat. fat), 22 mg chol., 80 mg sodium, 11 g carbo., 1 g fiber, 2 g pro.

To Make Ahead: Bake cookies as directed and cool completely. Place in a freezer container or bag and freeze up to 3 months. Before serving, thaw cookies about 15 minutes.

Black Walnut Pinwheels

Black walnuts may be tough nuts to crack, but true devotees of these intensely flavored nuts find opening them and picking out the meat well worth the effort.

Prep: 30 minutes   **Bake:** 7 to 9 minutes   **Chill:** 4 to 5 hours   **Oven:** 375°   **Makes:** 48

½ cup shortening
½ cup packed brown sugar
¾ teaspoon baking soda
¼ teaspoon salt
1 egg
1¾ cups all-purpose flour
⅓ cup butter, melted
⅔ cup packed brown sugar
½ teaspoon black walnut flavoring (optional)
1 cup finely ground black walnuts

1 In a large mixing bowl beat shortening with an electric mixer on medium to high speed for 30 seconds. Add the ½ cup brown sugar, baking soda, and salt; beat until combined, scraping sides of bowl occasionally. Beat in egg until combined. Beat in as much of the flour as you can with the mixer. Using a wooden spoon, stir in any remaining flour. Cover and chill dough for 1 to 2 hours or until firm enough to handle.

2 Meanwhile, combine melted butter, the ⅔ cup brown sugar, walnut flavoring (if desired), and walnuts.

3 On a lightly floured surface, roll dough into a 12-inch square. Spread walnut mixture evenly over dough; roll up jelly-roll style; seal edges. Wrap in plastic wrap. Chill in the refrigerator at least 3 hours.

4 Using a sharp knife, cut dough into ¼-inch slices. Place slices 2 inches apart on an ungreased cookie sheet.

5 Bake in a 375° oven for 7 to 9 minutes or until edges are light brown. Cool on baking sheet for 1 minute. Transfer cookies to a wire rack; cool.

Nutrition Facts per cookie: 84 cal., 5 g total fat (2 g sat. fat), 8 mg chol., 49 mg sodium, 9 g carbo., 1 g fiber, 1 g pro.

To Make Ahead: Bake cookies as directed and cool completely. Place in a freezer container or bag and freeze up to 3 months. Before serving, thaw cookies about 15 minutes.

Chocolate Ribbon Cookies

These striped cookies are perfect for any occasion. Pair them with a frosty glass of milk for an after-school snack or a demitasse of espresso for a sophisticated dessert.

Prep: 30 minutes   **Bake:** 10 minutes   **Oven:** 375°   **Makes:** 54

½ cup butter, softened
½ cup shortening
1 cup granulated sugar
½ teaspoon baking soda
⅛ teaspoon salt
1 egg
2 tablespoons milk
1 teaspoon vanilla
3 cups all-purpose flour
⅓ cup semisweet chocolate
    pieces, melted and
    cooled
½ cup finely chopped nuts
½ cup miniature semisweet
    chocolate pieces
¼ teaspoon rum flavoring

1 In a large mixing bowl beat butter and shortening with an electric mixer on medium to high speed for 30 seconds. Add sugar, baking soda, and salt; beat until combined, scraping sides of bowl occasionally. Beat in the egg, milk, and vanilla until combined. Beat in as much of the flour as you can with the mixer. Using a wooden spoon, stir in any remaining flour.

2 Divide dough in half. Knead the melted chocolate and nuts into half of the dough. Knead the miniature chocolate pieces and rum flavoring into the other half of dough. Divide each portion of dough in half.

3 To shape dough, line the bottom and sides of a 9×5×3-inch loaf pan with plastic wrap or waxed paper. Press half of the chocolate dough evenly into the pan. Top with half of the vanilla dough, then remaining chocolate dough, then remaining vanilla dough, pressing each layer firmly and evenly over the last layer.

4 Invert pan to remove dough. Peel off plastic wrap or waxed paper. Using a sharp knife, cut dough crosswise into thirds. Slice each third crosswise into ¼-inch slices. Place cookies 2 inches apart on an ungreased cookie sheet.

5 Bake in a 375° oven about 10 minutes or until edges are firm and bottoms are lightly browned. Transfer the cookies to a wire rack; cool.

Nutrition Facts per cookie: 100 cal., 6 g total fat (2 g sat. fat), 7 mg chol., 31 mg sodium, 10 g carbo., 1 g fiber, 1 g pro.

To Make Ahead: Bake cookies as directed and cool completely. Place in a freezer container or bag and freeze up to 3 months. Before serving, thaw cookies about 15 minutes.

Mint Swirls

Crushed chocolate sandwich cookies make an easy filling to swirl through these mint-spiked cookies. Tinted a delicate shade of green, they're perfect for St. Patrick's Day.

Prep: 30 minutes **Bake:** 8 to 9 minutes **Chill:** 5 hours **Oven:** 375° **Makes:** 50

¾ cup butter, softened
1 cup granulated sugar
1 teaspoon baking powder
1 egg
¼ teaspoon mint extract
   Few drops green food coloring
2¼ cups all-purpose flour
½ cup finely crushed chocolate sandwich cookies with white filling (about 6 cookies)
½ cup semisweet chocolate pieces (optional)
1 teaspoon shortening (optional)

1 In a large mixing bowl beat butter with an electric mixer on medium to high speed for 30 seconds. Add sugar and baking powder; beat until combined, scraping sides of bowl occasionally. Beat in egg, mint extract, and enough food coloring to tint dough light to medium green. Beat in as much of the flour as you can with the mixer. Using a wooden spoon, stir in any remaining flour. Divide dough in half. Cover and chill about 1 hour or until easy to handle.

2 Between 2 sheets of waxed paper, roll one portion of dough into an 8×7-inch rectangle. Peel off top sheet of waxed paper. Sprinkle half of crushed cookies evenly over dough to within ¼ inch of all sides. Starting from one of the short sides, roll up, jelly-roll style, removing bottom sheet of waxed paper as you roll; seal edges. Repeat with remaining dough and crushed cookies. Wrap rolls in plastic wrap or waxed paper. Chill about 4 hours or until firm.

3 Remove one roll of dough from the refrigerator. Unwrap and reshape slightly, if necessary. Using a sharp knife, cut dough into ¼-inch slices. Place slices 2 inches apart on an ungreased cookie sheet.

4 Bake in a 375° oven for 8 to 9 minutes or until edges are firm. Cool on cookie sheet for 1 minute. Transfer cookies to a wire rack; cool. Repeat with remaining roll of dough. If desired, in a heavy saucepan melt chocolate and shortening over low heat; drizzle over cooled cookies.

Nutrition Facts per cookie: 68 cal., 3 g total fat (2 g sat. fat), 12 mg chol., 48 mg sodium, 9 g carbo., 0 g fiber, 1 g pro.

To Make Ahead: Bake and cool cookies as directed, but do not drizzle with chocolate. Place in a freezer container or bag and freeze up to 3 months. Thaw cookies about 15 minutes. If desired, drizzle cookies with chocolate.

Maple Logs

These cookies show how easy it is to transform dough into fun objects. To shape the cookies, roll the dough into ropes and cut into logs. To create rough-hewn bark, pull a fork through the frosting.

Prep: 25 minutes   **Bake:** 8 to 10 minutes   **Chill:** 1 hour   **Oven:** 375°   **Makes:** 48

¾   cup butter, softened
¾   cup packed brown sugar
½   teaspoon salt
1   egg
1½ teaspoons maple flavoring
2   cups all-purpose flour
1   recipe Maple Frosting

1 In a large mixing bowl beat butter with an electric mixer on medium to high speed for 30 seconds. Add brown sugar and salt. Beat until combined, scraping sides of bowl occasionally. Beat in egg and maple flavoring until combined. Beat in as much flour as you can with the mixer. Using a wooden spoon, stir in any remaining flour. Cover dough and chill in the refrigerator about 1 hour or until easy to handle.

2 Divide dough into eight portions. On a lightly floured surface, roll each portion into a rope ½ inch in diameter. Cut ropes into logs about 3 inches long. Place on ungreased cookie sheet.

3 Bake in a 375° oven for 8 to 10 minutes or until golden. Transfer cookies to a wire rack; cool completely. Spread cookies with Maple Frosting. Pull tines of fork through frosting so it resembles bark.

Maple Frosting: In a small mixing bowl beat ¼ cup butter for 30 seconds. Gradually add 1½ cups sifted powdered sugar, beating well. Beat in 3 tablespoons milk and 1 teaspoon maple flavoring. Gradually beat in an additional 1½ to 1¾ cups sifted powdered sugar to make spreading consistency.

Nutrition Facts per cookie: 93 cal., 4 g total fat (3 g sat. fat), 15 mg chol., 69 mg sodium, 13 g carbo., 1 g fiber, 1 g pro.

To Make Ahead: Bake and cool cookies as directed, but do not frost. Place in a freezer container or bag and freeze up to 3 months. Thaw cookies about 15 minutes. Prepare frosting and spread over thawed cookies.

Toasted Coconut Wafers

Each crisp, buttery bite celebrates the sweet taste of coconut. Shredded coconut is stirred into the dough, and then the rolls of dough are coated with more coconut.

Prep: 25 minutes   **Bake:** 10 to 12 minutes   **Chill:** 4 to 24 hours   **Oven:** 375°   **Makes:** 60

  1   cup butter, softened
1¼   cups sifted powdered
        sugar
  ½   teaspoon almond extract
        or vanilla
  ⅛   teaspoon salt
  1   egg yolk
2¼   cups all-purpose flour
  1   cup shredded coconut,
        toasted
  1   beaten egg white
1½   cups shredded coconut

1 In a large mixing bowl beat butter with an electric mixer on medium to high speed for 30 seconds. Add powdered sugar, almond extract or vanilla, and salt; beat until combined, scraping sides of bowl occasionally. Beat in egg yolk. Beat in as much of the flour as you can with the mixer. Using a wooden spoon, stir in any remaining flour and the 1 cup toasted coconut.

2 Divide dough in half. Shape each half of dough into an 8-inch-long roll. Brush rolls with egg white and roll in the 1½ cups coconut. Wrap rolls in plastic wrap or waxed paper. Chill in refrigerator for 4 to 24 hours or until firm.

3 Using a sharp knife, cut dough into ¼-inch slices. Place slices 1 inch apart on an ungreased cookie sheet.

4 Bake in a 375° oven for 10 to 12 minutes or until edges are light brown. Cool on cookie sheet for 1 minute. Transfer cookies to a wire rack; cool.

Nutrition Facts per cookie: 68 cal., 4 g total fat (2 g sat. fat), 12 mg chol., 14 mg sodium, 7 g carbo., 0 g fiber, 1 g pro.

To Make Ahead: Bake cookies as directed and cool completely. Place in a freezer container or bag and freeze up to 3 months. Before serving, thaw cookies about 15 minutes.

Butterfly Cookies

The translucent colors of candied pineapple and papaya delicately color the wings of these cookie butterflies. Look for the candied fruit in specialty shops or large grocery stores.

Prep: 40 minutes   **Bake:** 6 minutes   **Chill:** 3 to 4 hours   **Oven:** 375°   **Makes:** 60

¾   cup butter, softened
½   cup granulated sugar
¼   cup packed brown sugar
¼   teaspoon baking powder
⅛   teaspoon baking soda
⅛   teaspoon salt
1   egg
½   teaspoon almond extract
1¾ cups all-purpose flour
½   cup chopped candied
      pineapple
½   cup chopped candied
      papaya
¼   cup semisweet chocolate
      pieces
¼   teaspoon shortening

1 In a large mixing bowl beat butter with an electric mixer on medium to high speed for 30 seconds. Add granulated sugar, brown sugar, baking powder, baking soda, and salt; beat until combined, scraping sides of bowl occasionally. Beat in egg and almond extract until combined. Beat in as much of the flour as you can with the mixer. Using a wooden spoon, stir in candied pineapple, candied papaya, and any remaining flour.

2 If dough is too sticky to handle, cover and chill in refrigerator for 1 to 2 hours or until easy to handle. Divide dough in half. Shape each half of dough into a 9-inch-long roll. Wrap rolls in plastic wrap or waxed paper. Chill about 2 hours or until firm.

3 Using a sharp knife, cut dough into ¼-inch slices. Cut each slice in half. Place rounded sides of two halves together on an ungreased cookie sheet, forming a butterfly.

4 Bake in a 375° oven about 6 minutes or until edges just begin to brown. Transfer cookies to a wire rack; cool completely. In a small saucepan combine chocolate and shortening; heat and stir over low heat until melted. Cool slightly. Spoon into a small, self-sealing plastic bag; seal bag. Snip a tiny piece off one corner of the bag. Pipe a chocolate butterfly body onto each cookie.

Nutrition Facts per cookie: 56 cal., 3 g total fat (1 g sat. fat), 7 mg chol., 32 mg sodium, 7 g carbo., 0 g fiber, 0 g pro.

To Make Ahead: Bake and cool cookies as directed, but do not apply chocolate butterfly body. Place in a freezer container or bag and freeze up to 3 months. Thaw cookies about 15 minutes. Pipe chocolate butterfly body onto thawed cookies.

Café Brûlot Cookies

At least one cup of café brûlot—a flaming drink of coffee, spices, citrus peels, and brandy—is a must for every visitor to New Orleans. We adapted the flavor to these crisp slice-and-bake cookies.

Prep: 20 minutes **Bake:** 7 to 8 minutes **Chill:** 2 hours **Oven:** 375° **Makes:** 48

1 cup packed brown sugar
½ cup pecan pieces
1 teaspoon instant coffee crystals
½ teaspoon ground cinnamon
¼ teaspoon ground cloves
½ cup butter
1 tablespoon finely shredded lemon peel
1 tablespoon finely shredded orange peel
1 tablespoon brandy or milk
1 egg yolk
1¾ cups all-purpose flour
1 recipe Brandy Icing

1 In a food processor bowl combine brown sugar, pecans, coffee crystals, cinnamon, and cloves. Cover and process until nuts are finely chopped. Add butter, lemon peel, and orange peel; process until butter is evenly mixed. Add brandy or milk and egg yolk; process until combined. Add flour gradually, processing until combined.

2 Divide dough in half. Shape each half into a 6 inch-long roll. Wrap rolls in plastic wrap or waxed paper. Chill in the refrigerator about 2 hours or until firm.

3 Using a sharp knife, cut dough into ¼-inch slices. Place slices 1½ inches apart on an ungreased cookie sheet.

4 Bake in a 375° oven for 7 to 8 minutes or until light brown. Transfer cookies to a wire rack; cool. Pipe or drizzle cooled cookies with Brandy Icing.

Brandy Icing: In a small bowl combine 1 cup sifted powdered sugar, ½ teaspoon vanilla, and 1 tablespoon brandy or strong coffee. Add milk, 1 teaspoon at a time, to make desired consistency.

Nutrition Facts per cookie: 69 cal., 3 g total fat (1 g sat. fat), 10 mg chol., 23 mg sodium, 10 g carbo., 0 g fiber, 1 g pro.

To Make Ahead: Bake and cool cookies as directed, but do not pipe with icing. Place in a freezer container or bag and freeze up to 3 months. Thaw cookies about 15 minutes. Prepare icing and pipe onto thawed cookies.

Shaped Cookies

Tropical Pinwheels

In this Chapter:

Snickerdoodles

These crackly topped cookies originated in New England although it's anyone's guess as to why they're called snickerdoodles. But they've long been a favorite of both young and old.

Prep: 25 minutes **Bake:** 10 to 11 minutes **Chill:** 1 hour **Oven:** 375° **Makes:** 36

½ cup butter, softened
1 cup granulated sugar
¼ teaspoon baking soda
¼ teaspoon cream of tartar
1 egg
½ teaspoon vanilla
1½ cups all-purpose flour
2 tablespoons granulated
 sugar
1 teaspoon ground
 cinnamon

1 In a medium mixing bowl beat butter with an electric mixer on medium to high speed for 30 seconds. Add the 1 cup sugar, baking soda, and cream of tartar; beat until combined, scraping sides of bowl occasionally. Beat in egg and vanilla until combined. Beat in as much of the flour as you can with the mixer. Using a wooden spoon, stir in any remaining flour. Cover and chill in the refrigerator for 1 hour.

2 In a small bowl combine the 2 tablespoons sugar and the cinnamon. Shape dough into 1-inch balls. Roll balls in the sugar-cinnamon mixture to coat. Place 2 inches apart on an ungreased cookie sheet.

3 Bake in a 375° oven for 10 to 11 minutes or until edges are golden brown. Transfer cookies to a wire rack; cool.

Nutrition Facts per cookie: 66 cal., 3 g total fat (2 g sat. fat), 13 mg chol., 36 mg sodium, 10 g carbo., 0 g fiber, 1 g pro.

To Make Ahead: Bake cookies as directed; cool completely. Place in a freezer container or bag and freeze for up to 3 months. Before serving, thaw for 15 minutes.

perfect cookie shapes

Never shortcut the chilling. I've found the key to perfectly shaped cookies is to chill the dough thoroughly before shaping. Chilled dough is easier to mold and helps the cookies better keep their shapes during baking.

Be sure to follow the recipe directions for chilling the dough. If you're working in a warm kitchen, return the dough to the refrigerator between batches. Some doughs, even when chilled, tend to stick to your hands. When shaping these doughs, dust your hands lightly with flour as necessary.

Maryellyn Krantz

Test Kitchen Home Economist

Frosty Snowballs

Edible glitter transforms a batch of these classic cookies into a colorful rainbow. Look for edible glitter in specialty shops or purchase it through mail-order houses.

Prep: 20 minutes   **Bake:** 20 minutes   **Oven:** 325°   **Makes:** 36

1 cup butter, softened
⅓ cup granulated sugar
1 tablespoon water
1 teaspoon vanilla
2¼ cups all-purpose flour
1 cup chopped pecans
1 cup sifted powdered sugar
   Green, pink, and purple edible cake sparkles or colored sugar

1 In a large mixing bowl beat butter with an electric mixer on medium to high speed for 30 seconds. Add the granulated sugar; beat until combined, scraping sides of bowl occasionally. Beat in water and vanilla until combined. Beat in as much of the flour as you can with the mixer. Using a wooden spoon, stir in any remaining flour and the chopped pecans.

2 Shape dough into 1-inch balls. Place 1 inch apart on an ungreased cookie sheet.

3 Bake in a 325° oven 20 minutes or until bottoms are light brown. Transfer cookies to a wire rack; cool completely.

4 In each of three small bowls place ⅓ cup of the sifted powdered sugar. Add a different color of edible cake sparkles or colored sugar to each bowl. Gently roll and shake cooled cookies in desired powdered sugar mixture.

Nutrition Facts per cookie: 110 cal., 7 g total fat (3 g sat. fat), 14 mg chol., 52 mg sodium, 11 g carbo., 0 g fiber, 1 g pro.

Crackled Sugar Cookies

These cookies bake longer and at a lower temperature than most other cookies. To keep them tender to the bite, don't let them brown.

Prep: 25 minutes   **Bake:** 20 minutes   **Oven:** 300°   **Makes:** 48

½ cup butter, softened
½ cup shortening
2 cups granulated sugar
1 teaspoon baking soda
1 teaspoon cream of tartar
⅛ teaspoon salt
3 egg yolks
½ teaspoon vanilla
2 cups all-purpose flour

1 In a large mixing bowl beat butter and shortening with an electric mixer on medium to high speed for 30 seconds. Add sugar, baking soda, cream of tartar, and salt; beat until combined, scraping sides of bowl occasionally. Beat in egg yolks and vanilla until combined. Beat in as much of the flour as you can with the mixer. Using a wooden spoon, stir in any remaining flour.

2 Shape dough into 1-inch balls. Place 2 inches apart on an ungreased cookie sheet.

3 Bake in a 300° oven about 20 minutes or until tops are slightly crackled and sides are set (do not let edges brown). Transfer cookies to a wire rack; cool.

Nutrition Facts per cookie: 90 cal., 5 g total fat (1 g sat. fat), 16 mg chol., 50 mg sodium, 12 g carbo., 0 g fiber, 1 g pro.

To Make Ahead: Bake cookies as directed; cool completely. Place in a freezer container or bag and freeze for up to 3 months. Before serving, thaw for 15 minutes.

gifts of cookies and tea

Whether you munch cookies by the handful or nibble daintily on one, a beverage makes them taste even better. And we all have our favorite snack-time beverage—coffee, tea, or hot chocolate. To personalize a cookie gift, pack the cookies with a mug or tea cup and add a small package of gourmet coffee, a packet of herbal tea bags, or a container of cocoa mix. For those who prefer cold beverages, fill a tall glass with cookies and pack with iced tea or lemonade mix.

Giant Ginger Cookies

Chewy and delicious, these cookies are giants in both size and snappy ginger flavor. And with their large size and robust flavor, they're the perfect dessert for a brown-bag lunch.

Prep: 20 minutes   **Bake:** 12 to 14 minutes   **Oven:** 350°   **Makes:** 25

4½ cups all-purpose flour
4 teaspoons ground ginger
2 teaspoons baking soda
1½ teaspoons ground
        cinnamon
1 teaspoon ground cloves
¼ teaspoon salt
1½ cups shortening
2 cups granulated sugar
2 eggs
½ cup molasses
¾ cup coarse sugar or
        granulated sugar

1 In a medium bowl stir together flour, ginger, baking soda, cinnamon, cloves, and salt; set aside.

2 In a large mixing bowl beat shortening with an electric mixer on low speed for 30 seconds to soften. Add the 2 cups granulated sugar; beat until combined, scraping sides of bowl occasionally. Beat in eggs and molasses until combined. Beat in as much of the flour mixture as you can with the mixer. Using a wooden spoon, stir in any remaining flour mixture.

3 Shape dough into 2-inch balls using ¼ cup dough (or measure dough using a #20 ice cream scoop). Roll balls in the ¾ cup coarse or granulated sugar. Place about 2½ inches apart on an ungreased cookie sheet.

4 Bake in a 350° oven for 12 to 14 minutes or until cookies are light brown and puffed. (Do not overbake.) Cool on cookie sheet for 2 minutes. Transfer cookies to a wire rack; cool.

Nutrition Facts per cookie: 293 cal., 13 g total fat (3 g sat. fat), 17 mg chol., 129 mg sodium, 42 g carbo., 1 g fiber, 3 g pro.

Chocolate-Covered Cherry Cookies

For these fudgy treats, you spread the frosting on the cookies before baking. Be sure to use real chocolate (not imitation) so the cookies will bake properly.

Prep: 30 minutes **Bake:** 10 minutes **Oven:** 350° **Makes:** 48

1½ **cups all-purpose flour**
½ **cup unsweetened cocoa powder**
½ **cup butter, softened**
1 **cup granulated sugar**
¼ **teaspoon baking soda**
¼ **teaspoon baking powder**
¼ **teaspoon salt**
1 **egg**
1½ **teaspoons vanilla**
48 **undrained maraschino cherries (about one 10-ounce jar)**
1 **cup (6 ounces) semisweet chocolate pieces**
½ **cup sweetened condensed milk**

1 In a medium bowl mix flour and cocoa powder; set aside. In a large mixing bowl beat butter with an electric mixer on medium to high speed for 30 seconds. Add sugar, baking soda, baking powder, and salt; beat until combined, scraping sides of bowl occasionally. Beat in egg and vanilla until combined. Beat in as much of the flour mixture as you can with the mixer. Using a wooden spoon, stir in any remaining flour mixture.

2 Shape dough into 1-inch balls. Place 2 inches apart on an ungreased cookie sheet. Press down center of each ball with your thumb. Drain maraschino cherries, reserving juice. Place a cherry in the center of each cookie.

3 For frosting, in a small saucepan combine chocolate pieces and sweetened condensed milk; heat until chocolate is melted. Stir in 4 teaspoons of the reserved cherry juice. Spoon about 1 teaspoon of frosting over each cherry, spreading to cover cherry. If necessary, thin frosting with additional cherry juice.

4 Bake in a 350° oven about 10 minutes or until sides are set. Transfer cookies to a wire rack; cool.

Nutrition Facts per cookie: 81 cal., 3 g total fat (1 g sat. fat), 11 mg chol., 45 mg sodium, 12 g carbo., 0 g fiber, 1 g pro.

To Make Ahead: Bake cookies as directed; cool completely. Place in a freezer container or bag and freeze for up to 3 months. Before serving, thaw for 15 minutes.

Chocolate Crinkles

These easy-mix cookies taste like sugar-coated brownies. They taste even better when served with big bowls of ice cream.

Prep: 30 minutes   **Bake:** 8 to 10 minutes   **Chill:** 1 to 2 hours   **Oven:** 375°   **Makes:** 48

3 eggs
1½ cups granulated sugar
4 ounces unsweetened chocolate, melted
½ cup cooking oil
2 teaspoons baking powder
2 teaspoons vanilla
2 cups all-purpose flour
Sifted powdered sugar

1 In a large mixing bowl beat eggs, granulated sugar, chocolate, cooking oil, baking powder, and vanilla with an electric mixer on medium to high speed until combined, scraping sides of bowl occasionally. Beat in as much of the flour as you can with the mixer. Using a wooden spoon, stir in any remaining flour. Cover; chill in the refrigerator for 1 to 2 hours or until easy to handle. Shape into 1-inch balls. Roll balls in powdered sugar to coat generously. Place 1 inch apart on an ungreased cookie sheet.

2 Bake in a 375° oven for 8 to 10 minutes or until edges are set and tops are crackled. Transfer cookies to a wire rack; cool completely. If desired, sprinkle with additional powdered sugar.

Nutrition Facts per cookie: 80 cal., 4 g total fat (1 g sat. fat), 13 mg chol., 19 mg sodium, 11 g carbo., 0 g fiber, 1 g pro.

To Make Ahead: Bake and cool cookies as directed. Do not sprinkle with powdered sugar. Place in a freezer container; freeze for up to 3 months. Thaw about 15 minutes. If desired, sprinkle thawed cookies with powdered sugar.

melting chocolate

Melting chocolate requires a little patience and extra care. If using chocolate squares, coarsely chop the chocolate before melting. If melting over direct heat, put the chocolate in a heavy-bottomed saucepan over the lowest heat. Using a wooden spoon, stir constantly until the chocolate just begins to melt. Remove the saucepan from the heat and continue stirring until smooth. If necessary, return to heat for only a few seconds.

If you use a microwave, cook the chopped chocolate, uncovered, only until soft. Stir it often to keep the heat evenly distributed through the chocolate. For 4 ounces of chopped chocolate, allow 1 to 2 minutes, stirring after 1 minute and then stirring every 30 seconds.

Chocolate-Mint Creams

Candy mint kisses make a super-easy frosting in a variety of pastel colors for these chocolate cookies. Look for the mints at candy shops, department store candy counters, or food gift shops.

Prep: 25 minutes **Bake:** 10 minutes **Chill:** 1 to 2 hours **Oven:** 350° **Makes:** 48

1¼ cups all-purpose flour
½ teaspoon baking soda
⅔ cup packed brown sugar
6 tablespoons butter
1 tablespoon water
1 cup (6 ounces) semisweet
   chocolate pieces
1 egg
8 to 12 ounces pastel cream
   mint kisses

1 In a small bowl stir together flour and baking soda; set aside. In a medium saucepan cook and stir brown sugar, butter, and water over low heat until butter is melted. Add chocolate pieces. Cook and stir until chocolate is melted. Pour into a large mixing bowl; let stand for 10 to 15 minutes or until cool.

2 Using a wooden spoon, beat egg into chocolate mixture. Stir in the flour mixture until well mixed. (Dough will be soft.) Cover and chill in the refrigerator for 1 to 2 hours or until dough is easy to handle.

3 Shape dough into 1-inch balls. Place balls 2 inches apart on an ungreased cookie sheet.

4 Bake in a 350° oven for 8 minutes. Remove from oven and immediately top each cookie with a mint kiss. Return to the oven and bake about 2 minutes more or until edges are set. Swirl the melted mints with a knife to "frost" cookies. Transfer cookies to a wire rack; cool.

Nutrition Facts per cookie: 76 cal., 4 g total fat (2 g sat. fat), 8 mg chol., 34 mg sodium, 10 g carbo., 0 g fiber, 1 g pro.

Orange and Nut Cookies

The rich buttery taste of macadamia nuts paired with zesty orange peel gives these cookies an exquisite flavor.

Prep: 35 minutes **Bake:** 12 to 15 minutes **Oven:** 350° **Makes:** 72

4 cups all-purpose flour
2 cups sifted powdered
  sugar
1 cup cornstarch
2 cups butter
1 cup chopped macadamia
  nuts or toasted walnuts
2 beaten egg yolks
1 tablespoon finely
  shredded orange peel
4 to 6 tablespoons orange
  juice
  Granulated sugar
1 recipe Orange Frosting
  Finely shredded orange
  peel (optional)

1 In a large mixing bowl stir together flour, powdered sugar, and cornstarch. Using a pastry blender, cut in butter until mixture resembles coarse crumbs. Stir in nuts. In a bowl combine egg yolks, the 1 tablespoon orange peel, and 4 tablespoons of the orange juice; add to flour mixture, stirring until moistened. If necessary, add enough of the remaining orange juice to moisten.

2 On a lightly floured surface, knead dough until it forms a ball. Shape dough into 1¼-inch balls. Place balls about 2 inches apart on an ungreased cookie sheet. Using the bottom of a glass dipped in granulated sugar, flatten balls to ¼-inch thickness.

3 Bake in a 350° oven for 12 to 15 minutes or until edges begin to brown. Transfer cookies to a wire rack; cool completely. Spread cooled cookies with Orange Frosting. If desired, garnish with finely shredded orange peel.

Orange Frosting: In a small bowl stir together 2 cups sifted powdered sugar, 3 tablespoons softened butter, 1 teaspoon finely shredded orange peel, and enough orange juice (2 to 3 tablespoons) to make of spreading consistency.

Nutrition Facts per cookie: 120 cal., 7 g total fat (2 g sat. fat), 13 mg chol., 56 mg sodium, 13 g carbo., 0 g fiber, 1 g pro.

To Make Ahead: Bake and cool cookies as directed, but do not frost. Place in a freezer container or bag and freeze for up to 3 months. Thaw cookies in container about 15 minutes. Prepare frosting and spread over cooled cookies.

Peanut Butter and Candy Cookies

Wrap honey-sweetened, peanutty cookie dough around bite-size candy bars to create two treats in one. If miniature candy bars aren't available, cut regular-size bars into 1-inch squares.

Prep: 25 minutes   **Bake:** 12 to 15 minutes   **Oven:** 350°   **Makes:** 24

1¾ cups all-purpose flour
½ cup granulated sugar
½ teaspoon baking soda
¼ teaspoon salt
½ cup butter
½ cup creamy peanut butter
¼ cup honey
1 tablespoon milk
24 miniature chocolate-coated caramel-topped nougat bars with peanuts

1 In a large mixing bowl stir together flour, sugar, baking soda, and salt. Using a pastry blender, cut in the butter and peanut butter until mixture resembles coarse crumbs. Using a wooden spoon, beat in honey and milk until well combined.

2 For each cookie, pat 1 tablespoon of the dough into a 2-inch circle. Place 1 piece of candy in the center of the circle. Shape the dough around candy to form a 1½-inch ball. Place the balls 2 inches apart on an ungreased cookie sheet.

3 Bake in a 350° oven for 12 to 15 minutes or until edges are light brown. Transfer cookies to a wire rack; cool.

Nutrition Facts per cookie: 148 cal., 8 g total fat (3 g sat. fat), 11 mg chol., 125 mg sodium, 17 g carbo., 1 g fiber, 3 g pro.

Peanut Butter Cookies: Mix dough as directed. Shape into 1-inch balls. Roll in additional granulated sugar to coat. Place 2 inches apart on an ungreased cookie sheet. Flatten by making crisscross marks with the tines of a fork. Bake and cool as directed.

Nutrition Facts per cookie: 125 cal., 7 g total fat (3 g sat. fat), 11 mg chol., 117 mg sodium, 14 g carbo., 1 g fiber, 2 g pro.

To Make Ahead: Bake cookies as directed; cool completely. Place in a freezer container or bag and freeze for up to 3 months. Before serving, thaw for 15 minutes.

Shortbread

We have Scotland to thank for these rich, buttery cookies. According to Scottish tradition, the scallops on the edges represent the rays of the sun.

Prep: 15 minutes **Bake:** 25 to 30 minutes **Oven:** 325° **Makes:** 16

1¼ cups all-purpose flour
3 tablespoons granulated
    sugar
½ cup butter

1 In a medium bowl combine flour and sugar. Cut in butter until mixture resembles fine crumbs and starts to cling together. Form the mixture into a ball and knead until smooth.

2 Pat or roll dough into an 8-inch circle on an ungreased cookie sheet. Press edge with your fingers to scallop. Cut the circle into 16 wedges; leave wedges adjoining in the circle. Prick each wedge with a fork.

3 Bake in a 325° oven for 25 to 30 minutes or until the bottom just starts to brown and center is set. Cut circle into wedges again while warm. Cool on the cookie sheet for 5 minutes. Transfer to a wire rack; cool. Makes 16 wedges.

Nutrition Facts per cookie: 95 cal., 6 g total fat (4 g sat. fat), 16 mg chol., 62 mg sodium, 9 g carbo., 0 g fiber, 1 g pro.

Cornmeal Shortbread: Prepare as directed, except reduce all-purpose flour to 1 cup. Add ¼ cup cornmeal to the flour mixture. After cutting in the butter, stir in ¼ cup snipped dried cranberries or dried cherries.

Lemon and Poppy Seed Shortbread: Prepare as directed, except stir 1 tablespoon poppy seed into the flour mixture and add 1 teaspoon finely shredded lemon peel with the butter.

Spiced Shortbread: Prepare as directed, except substitute brown sugar for the granulated sugar. Stir ½ teaspoon ground cinnamon, ¼ teaspoon ground ginger, and ⅛ teaspoon ground cloves into the flour mixture.

To Make Ahead: Bake cookies as directed; cool completely. Place in a freezer container or bag and freeze for up to 3 months. Before serving, thaw for 15 minutes.

Chocolate Chip Cookie Sticks

With a biscotti-like texture, this twice-baked version of America's favorite cookie is perfect for dunking in milk or coffee.

Prep: 35 minutes   **Bake:** 28 to 33 minutes   **Stand:** 1 hour   **Oven:** 375°/325°   **Makes:** 18

½ cup butter, softened
½ cup shortening
1 cup packed brown sugar
½ cup granulated sugar
½ teaspoon baking soda
2 eggs
2 teaspoons vanilla
2½ cups all-purpose flour
8 ounces coarsely chopped semisweet chocolate (2 cups)
1 cup chopped walnuts, pecans, or hazelnuts (filberts) (optional)

1 Line a 13×9×2-inch baking pan with foil; set aside. In a large mixing bowl beat butter and shortening with an electric mixer on medium to high speed for 30 seconds. Add brown sugar, granulated sugar, and baking soda; beat until combined, scraping sides of bowl occasionally. Beat in the eggs and vanilla until combined. Beat in as much of the flour as you can with the mixer. Using a wooden spoon, stir in any remaining flour. Stir in chocolate and, if desired, nuts. Press dough evenly into the prepared pan.

3 Bake in a 375° oven for 22 to 25 minutes or until golden brown and center is set. Cool in pan on a wire rack 1 hour.

4 Preheat oven to 325°. Holding securely to foil lining, gently remove cookies from pan and place on a cutting board, leaving cookies on foil lining. Cut crosswise into 9×½-inch slices. Place slices, cut side down, about 1 inch apart on an ungreased cookie sheet. Bake for 6 to 8 minutes or until cut edges are crispy. Carefully transfer cookies to wire rack (cookies will be tender). Cool.

Nutrition Facts per cookie: 333 cal., 20 g total fat (8 g sat. fat), 37 mg chol., 98 mg sodium, 39 g carbo., 2 g fiber, 4 g pro.

To Make Ahead: Bake cookies as directed; cool completely. Place in a freezer container or bag and freeze for up to 3 months. Before serving, thaw for 15 minutes.

Peanut Butter and Fudge Bites

You need just three ingredients to make these luscious tarts—refrigerated cookie dough, semisweet chocolate pieces, and sweetened condensed milk.

Prep: 20 minutes   **Bake:** 11 minutes   **Oven:** 350°   **Makes:** 24

Tart Shells
Nonstick cooking spray
½ of an 18-ounce roll
   refrigerated peanut
   butter cookie dough

Filling
½ cup semisweet chocolate
   pieces
¼ cup sweetened condensed
   milk

1 Lightly coat twenty-four 1¾-inch muffin cups with cooking spray; set aside.

2 For tart shells, cut cookie dough into 6 equal pieces. Cut each piece into four equal slices. Place each slice of dough in a prepared cup.

3 Bake in a 350° oven about 9 minutes or until edges are light brown and dough is slightly firm but not set. Remove tart shells from oven. Gently press a shallow indentation in each tart shell with the back of a round ½ teaspoon measuring spoon.

4 Bake 2 minutes more or until the edges of tart shells are firm and light golden brown. Let tart shells cool in cups on a wire rack for 15 minutes. Carefully remove tart shells from cups. Cool completely on wire racks.

5 For filling, in a small saucepan combine chocolate pieces and sweetened condensed milk. Cook and stir over medium heat until chocolate is melted. Spoon a slightly rounded teaspoon of filling into each cooled tart shell. Cool until filling to set.

Nutrition Facts per tart: 75 cal., 4 g total fat (1 g sat. fat), 4 mg chol., 46 mg sodium, 10 g carbo., 0 g fiber, 1 g pro.

party perfect

Easy to serve, Peanut Butter and Fudge Bites and Orange Curd Tarts make sweet additions to open-house buffet tables, potluck dinners, and other serve-yourself gatherings. To serve, place each tart in a decorative paper bake cup and arrange on a flat platter. Or, for gift-giving, place the tarts in paper bake cups and pack in a single layer in a decorative tin. Or, line a new muffin pan with the paper bake cups and put the tarts in the muffin cups. The recipient will be delighted with a sweet as well as useful gift.

Orange Curd Tarts

These dainty tarts, brimming with homemade orange curd, are equally fitting for a British high tea or an American-style coffee break.

Prep: 45 minutes **Bake:** 20 to 25 minutes **Oven:** 350° **Makes:** 32

Tart Shells
1 package pie crust mix
   (for 2 crusts)
¼ cup finely chopped pecans
⅓ cup cold water

Filling
1 cup granulated sugar
2 teaspoons cornstarch
1 tablespoon finely
   shredded orange peel
   (set aside)
⅓ cup orange juice
2 tablespoons butter, cut up
3 beaten eggs
½ cup coarsely chopped
   pecans (optional)
   Small orange peel curls
   (optional)

1 Lightly grease thirty-two 1¾-inch muffin pan cups; set aside. In a small bowl stir together pie crust mix and the ¼ cup finely chopped pecans. Add cold water and stir until moistened. Divide dough in half.

2 On a lightly floured surface, roll half of the dough at a time into a 10½-inch square; trim to a 10-inch square. Cut each square into sixteen 2½-inch squares. Fit squares into muffin cups, pleating sides and leaving corners standing up slightly.

3 For filling, in a medium saucepan combine sugar and cornstarch. Add orange juice and butter. Cook and stir over medium heat until thickened and bubbly. Cook and stir 2 minutes more. Stir about half of the juice mixture into beaten eggs. Return juice-egg mixture to saucepan. Remove from heat. Stir in finely shredded orange peel.

4 Spoon about 2 teaspoons orange mixture into each pastry-lined muffin cup. If desired, top each tart with a few coarsely chopped pecans.

5 Bake in a 350° oven for 20 to 25 minutes or until filling is set and crust is light brown. Cool in pans on wire rack for 20 minutes. Carefully remove from pans and transfer to wire rack; cool completely. If desired, garnish tops with a small orange peel curl just before serving.

Nutrition Facts per tart: 96 cal., 5 g total fat (1 g sat. fat), 22 mg chol., 81 mg sodium, 12 g carbo., 0 g fiber, 1 g pro.

Raspberry-Almond Ribbons

Shape the dough for this Scandinavian specialty into four long bars. Top the baked bars with raspberry preserves, sliced almonds, and vanilla icing before cutting them into dainty ribbons.

Prep: 30 minutes **Bake:** 12 to 14 minutes **Oven:** 325° **Makes:** 52

Dough
- ½ cup butter, softened
- 1 cup granulated sugar
- 2 teaspoons baking powder
- ¼ teaspoon salt
- 1 egg
- ¼ teaspoon almond extract
- 1¾ cups all-purpose flour

Toppings
- ½ cup seedless raspberry jam or apricot preserves
- ½ cup sliced almonds, toasted

Icing
- 1 cup sifted powdered sugar
- ¼ teaspoon vanilla
- 2 to 3 tablespoons milk

1 In a large mixing bowl beat butter with an electric mixer on medium speed for 30 seconds. Add granulated sugar, baking powder, and salt; beat until combined, scraping sides of bowl occasionally. Beat in egg and almond extract until combined. Beat in as much of the flour as you can with the mixer. Using a wooden spoon, stir in any remaining flour.

2 Divide dough into four equal portions. Shape each portion into a 13×2-inch rectangle on an ungreased baking sheet, placing rectangles 4 to 5 inches apart.

3 Bake in a 325° oven for 12 to 14 minutes or until edges are firm. Cool on baking sheets for 2 minutes. Carefully transfer to wire racks; cool completely.

4 Spread 2 tablespoons jam or preserves down center of each bar. Sprinkle almonds on both sides of the jam. For icing, stir together powdered sugar, vanilla, and enough milk to make of drizzling consistency. Drizzle icing across the top of each bar. Cut bars into 1-inch-wide strips.

Nutrition Facts per cookie: 71 cal., 3 g total fat (1 g sat. fat), 9 mg chol., 48 mg sodium, 11 g carbo., 0 g fiber, 1 g pro.

To Make Ahead: Bake and cool cookies as directed; do not add toppings or icing and do not cut into bars. Place in a freezer container or bag and freeze for up to 3 months. Thaw in containers about 1 hour. To serve, top with jam, almonds, and icing, and cut into bars as directed.

Nut Wedges

Reminiscent of Greek baklava, but so much easier to make, these tiny pastries are bursting with a rich honey-nut filling. Brew a pot of tea to serve with them.

Prep: 30 minutes   **Bake:** 15 to 20 minutes   **Oven:** 375°   **Makes:** 16 to 20

Pastry
1 package pie crust mix
    (for 2 crusts)
¼ cup granulated sugar
3 to 4 tablespoons water

Filling
1 cup finely chopped nuts
⅓ cup granulated sugar
2 tablespoons honey
1 teaspoon ground
    cinnamon
1 teaspoon lemon juice
    Milk

Drizzle
½ cup semisweet chocolate
    pieces
1 teaspoon shortening

1 In a medium bowl stir together pie crust mix and the ¼ cup sugar. Add enough water to form a ball. Divide dough in half.

2 On a lightly floured surface, roll each half of the dough into a 9-inch circle. Transfer 1 circle to an ungreased cookie sheet.

3 For filling, combine the nuts, the ⅓ cup sugar, honey, cinnamon, and lemon juice. Spread over dough circle on cookie sheet. Top with remaining dough circle. Use tines of fork to seal edges and prick dough. Brush with milk.

4 Bake in a 375° oven for 15 to 20 minutes or until pastry starts to brown. Cool 10 minutes on a wire rack. While warm, cut into 16 to 20 wedges. Cool completely.

5 In a small saucepan combine the chocolate pieces and shortening. Cook and stir over low heat just until melted. Drizzle over wedges.

Nutrition Facts per cookie: 214 cal., 13 g total fat (2 g sat. fat), 0 mg chol., 136 mg sodium, 24 g carbo., 1 g fiber, 3 g pro.

Pecan Snaps with Espresso Cream

These elegant, filled cones are truly a special occasion cookie. Prepare the coffee-spiked cream and pipe into the cookies just before serving. They're also delicious filled with plain whipped cream.

Prep: 35 minutes   **Bake:** 7 to 8 minutes per batch   **Oven:** 350°   **Makes:** 30

Batter

- ¼ cup packed brown sugar
- 3 tablespoons butter, melted
- 2 tablespoons dark-colored corn syrup
- 1 tablespoon coffee liqueur or coffee
- ½ cup finely chopped pecans
- ¼ cup all-purpose flour

Filling

- 1 cup whipping cream
- ¼ cup sifted powdered sugar
- 4 teaspoons instant espresso coffee powder
  Grated chocolate (optional)

1 Lightly grease a cookie sheet or line with foil. In a small bowl stir together brown sugar, melted butter, corn syrup, and coffee liqueur or coffee. Stir in pecans and flour until combined. Drop batter by level teaspoons 3 inches apart, or level tablespoons 5 inches apart, onto the prepared cookie sheet. (Bake only 4 or 5 cookies at a time.)

2 Bake in a 350° oven for 7 to 8 minutes for smaller cookies or 8 to 10 minutes for larger cookies or until cookies are bubbly and a deep golden brown.

3 Cool cookies on the cookie sheet for 1 to 2 minutes or until set. Quickly remove 1 cookie; roll cookie around a metal cone or the greased handle of a wooden spoon. When the cookie is firm, slide the cookie off the cone or spoon and cool completely on a wire rack. Repeat with remaining cookies, one at a time. (If cookies harden before you can shape them, reheat them in the oven about 1 minute or until softened.)

4 Up to 30 minutes before serving, in a large mixing bowl beat whipping cream, powdered sugar, and espresso coffee powder with an electric mixer on low speed until stiff peaks form. Pipe or spoon some of the whipped cream into each cookie. If desired, sprinkle with grated chocolate.

Nutrition Facts per filled cookie: 68 cal., 5 g total fat (3 g sat. fat), 14 mg chol., 16 mg sodium, 5 g carbo., 0 g fiber, 0 g pro.

To Make Ahead: Bake, shape, and cool cookies as directed. Arrange in a single layer in a freezer container and freeze for up to 1 month. To serve, thaw cookies for 15 minutes. Prepare the whipped cream mixture and fill the cookies as directed.

Lemon Tuiles

These light and lemony French cookies were named after roof tiles they're said to resemble. To shape the cookies into gentle curves, wrap the warm-from-the-oven cookies around a rolling pin.

Prep: 45 minutes **Bake:** 5 to 7 minutes **Oven:** 375° **Makes:** 24

2 egg whites
¼ cup butter, melted
2 teaspoons finely shredded
   lemon peel
¼ teaspoon lemon extract
½ cup sugar
½ cup all-purpose flour

1 In a medium mixing bowl let egg whites stand at room temperature for 30 minutes.

2 Line a cookie sheet with foil or parchment paper. Lightly grease foil-lined cookie sheet; set aside. Combine butter, lemon peel, and lemon extract; set aside.

3 Beat egg whites with an electric mixer on medium speed until soft peaks form (tips curl). Gradually add sugar, beating on high speed until stiff peaks form (tips stand straight). Fold in about half of the flour. Gently stir in butter mixture. Fold in remaining flour until thoroughly combined.

4 For each cookie, drop a level tablespoon of batter onto the prepared cookie sheet (bake only 3 or 4 cookies at a time). Using the back of a spoon, spread batter into 3-inch circles.

5 Bake in a 375° oven for 5 to 7 minutes or until cookies are golden brown around edges. Using a wide spatula, immediately remove the cookies and drape in a single layer over a standard-size rolling pin (place cookies with the side that was against the cookie sheet against the rolling pin). Cool cookies on rolling pin until they hold their shape; then carefully slide off rolling pin. Cool completely on a wire rack.

Nutrition Facts per cookie: 43 cal., 2 g total fat (1 g sat. fat), 5 mg chol., 11 mg sodium, 6 g carbo., 0 g fiber, 1 g pro.

To Make Ahead: Bake, shape, and cool cookies as directed. Arrange in a single layer in a freezer container and freeze for up to 1 month. To serve, thaw cookies for 15 minutes.

Tropical Pinwheels

Get set for tropical indulgence with these fun-to-shape cookies. They're bursting with pineapple, coconut, and buttery macadamia nuts.

Prep: 40 minutes **Bake:** 8 to 10 minutes **Chill:** 3 hours **Oven:** 350° **Makes:** 32

⅓ cup butter, softened
⅓ cup shortening
¾ cup granulated sugar
1½ teaspoons baking powder
¼ teaspoon salt
1 egg
4 teaspoons milk
1 teaspoon vanilla
2 cups all-purpose flour
1 3-ounce package cream
    cheese, softened
2 tablespoons granulated
    sugar
¼ cup coconut
¼ cup finely chopped
    macadamia nuts or
    almonds
    Colored sugar (optional)
    recipe Pineapple Icing
    (optional)

1 In a large mixing bowl beat butter and shortening with an electric mixer on medium to high speed 30 seconds. Add the ¾ cup sugar, the baking powder, and salt. Beat until combined, scraping sides of bowl occasionally. Beat in egg, milk, and vanilla until combined. Beat in as much of the flour as you can with the mixer. Using a wooden spoon, stir in any remaining flour.

2 Divide dough in half. Cover and chill the dough for 3 hours or until it is easy to handle.

3 For filling, in a small mixing bowl stir together cream cheese and the 2 tablespoons sugar. Stir in the coconut. Set aside.

4 On a lightly floured surface, roll half of the dough at a time into a 10-inch square. Using a fluted pastry wheel or a sharp knife, cut square into sixteen 2½-inch squares. Place squares 2 inches apart on an ungreased cookie sheet. Cut 1-inch slits from each corner toward the center of each square. Spoon a level teaspoon of the filling in each center. Fold every other tip to center to form a pinwheel, pressing lightly to seal the tips. Carefully sprinkle some of the chopped nuts onto the center of each pinwheel; press nuts lightly into the dough. If desired, sprinkle cookies with colored sugar.

5 Bake in a 350° oven for 8 to 10 minutes or until edges are light brown. Cool for 1 minute on cookie sheet. Transfer cookies to a wire rack; cool. If desired, drizzle cooled cookies with Pineapple Icing and sprinkle with additional colored sugar.

Pineapple Icing: In a small bowl, stir together ¾ cup sifted powdered sugar and enough pineapple juice (about 1 tablespoon) to make icing of drizzling consistency.

Nutrition Facts per cookie: 105 cal., 6 g total fat (3 g sat. fat), 15 mg chol., 63 mg sodium, 12 g carbo., 0 g fiber, 1 g pro.

Cutout Cookies

Sugar Cookie Cutouts

In this Chapter:

Sugar Cookie Cutouts

Decorative frosting applied to glazed sugar cookies creates a stunning two-tone trim. For best results, tint the frostings with paste food colorings available at specialty shops or through mail-order houses.

Prep: 45 minutes **Bake:** 7 to 8 minutes **Chill:** 3 hours **Oven:** 375° **Makes:** 36 to 48

⅓ cup butter, softened
⅓ cup shortening
¾ cup granulated sugar
1 teaspoon baking powder
Dash salt
1 egg
1 teaspoon vanilla
2 cups all-purpose flour
1 recipe Powdered Sugar Glaze
1 recipe Decorative Frosting

1 In a medium mixing bowl beat butter and shortening with an electric mixer on medium to high speed for 30 seconds. Add sugar, baking powder, and salt; beat until combined, scraping sides of bowl occasionally. Beat in egg and vanilla until combined. Beat in as much of the flour as you can with the mixer. Using a wooden spoon, stir in any remaining flour.

2 Divide dough in half. If necessary, cover and chill the dough for 3 hours or until it is easy to handle.

3 On a lightly floured surface, roll half of the dough at a time to ⅛-inch thickness. Using a 2½-inch cookie cutter, cut out dough. Place cutouts on an ungreased cookie sheet.

4 Bake in a 375° oven for 7 to 8 minutes or until edges are firm and bottoms are very light brown. Transfer cookies to a wire rack; cool completely.

5 To decorate, glaze with white or tinted Powdered Sugar Glaze. Let dry. Pipe dots or lines with white or tinted Decorative Frosting. Let dry. Or, for swirled tops, glaze cookies as above. Using 1 teaspoon milk at a time, thin some of the white or tinted Decorative Frosting until drizzling consistency. Scatter dots of thinned frosting on top of freshly glazed cookies. To swirl, pull wooden toothpick through dots. Let dry.

Powdered Sugar Glaze: In a mixing bowl combine 4 cups sifted powdered sugar and ¼ cup milk. Stir in additional milk, 1 teaspoon at a time, until glaze is easy to drizzle. Tint as desired with food coloring paste.

Decorative Frosting: In a mixing bowl stir together 4 cups sifted powdered sugar and 3 tablespoons milk until smooth. Stir in additional milk, 1 teaspoon at a time, until frosting is easy to pipe. Tint frosting as desired with food coloring paste.

Nutrition Facts per cookie: 74 cal., 4 g total fat (2 g sat. fat), 10 mg chol., 33 mg sodium, 9 g carbo., 0 g fiber, 1 g pro.

Pistachio Sugar Cookies

A dip in melted chocolate and a delicate flourish of melted candy coating transform these simple cookies into elegant tidbits.

Prep: 40 minutes **Bake:** 7 to 8 minutes **Chill:** 3 hours **Oven:** 375° **Makes:** 54 to 72

1 cup butter, softened
1 cup granulated sugar
1½ teaspoons baking powder
Dash salt
1 egg
3 tablespoons light cream or
milk
¼ teaspoon almond extract
3 cups all-purpose flour
½ cup ground pistachio nuts
Granulated sugar
6 ounces semisweet
chocolate, cut up
2 teaspoons shortening
1 ounce green or pink candy
coating, melted
(optional)

1 In a large mixing bowl beat butter with an electric mixer on medium to high speed for 30 seconds. Add the 1 cup sugar, baking powder, and salt; beat until combined, scraping sides of bowl occasionally. Beat in egg, light cream or milk, and almond extract until combined. Beat in as much of the flour as you can with the mixer. Using a wooden spoon, stir in any remaining flour and the ground nuts.

2 Divide dough into thirds. Cover and chill the dough for 3 hours or until it is easy to handle.

3 On a lightly floured surface, roll one portion of dough at a time to ⅛-inch thickness. Using a 2½- to 3-inch cookie cutter, cut out dough. Place cutouts on an ungreased cookie sheet. Sprinkle with additional sugar.

4 Bake in a 375° oven for 7 to 8 minutes or until edges are firm and bottoms are very light brown. Transfer cookies to a wire rack; cool completely.

5 In a heavy small saucepan melt chocolate and shortening over low heat, stirring constantly. Dip half of each cookie into melted chocolate; place on a wire rack over waxed paper until set. If desired, place melted candy coating in a heavy self-sealing plastic bag; seal. Snip off a corner of the bag. Drizzle coating in a loop design over chocolate-coated cookies. Let stand on the wire rack until set.

Nutrition Facts per cookie: 100 cal., 6 g total fat (3 g sat. fat), 14 mg chol., 52 mg sodium, 11 g carbo., 1 g fiber, 1 g pro.

To Make Ahead: Bake and cool cookies as directed, but do not decorate. Place in a freezer container or bag and freeze up to 3 months. Before serving, thaw cookies about 15 minutes. Decorate as directed.

Nutmeg Softies

If you like your sugar cookies big and soft, this is the recipe for you. Enjoy these old-fashioned cookies with a tall glass of ice-cold milk.

Prep: 35 minutes   **Bake:** 10 minutes   **Oven:** 350°   **Makes:** 32

½ cup butter, softened
½ cup shortening
1½ cups granulated sugar
1 teaspoon baking soda
1 teaspoon ground nutmeg
½ teaspoon salt
1 cup dairy sour cream
1 egg
1 teaspoon vanilla
4 cups all-purpose flour
   Colored coarse sugar

1 In a large mixing bowl beat butter and shortening with an electric mixer on medium to high speed 30 seconds. Add granulated sugar, soda, nutmeg, and salt; beat until combined, scraping sides of bowl occasionally. Beat in sour cream, egg, and vanilla until combined. Beat in as much of the flour as you can with the mixer. Using a wooden spoon, stir in any remaining flour (dough will be sticky). Divide dough into thirds. Cover and chill the dough for 2 hours or until it is easy to handle.

2 On a lightly floured surface, roll one portion of dough at a time to ¼-inch thickness. Using a floured 3-inch cookie cutter, cut out dough. Place cutouts on an ungreased cookie sheet. Sprinkle with colored sugar.

3 Bake in a 350° oven about 10 minutes or until edges of cookies are firm. Transfer cookies to a wire rack; cool.

Nutrition Facts per cookie: 160 cal., 8 g total fat (4 g sat. fat), 18 mg chol., 112 mg sodium, 21 g carbo., 1 g fiber, 2 g pro.

To Make Ahead: Bake cookies as directed and cool completely. Place in a freezer container or bag and freeze up to 3 months. Before serving, thaw cookies about 15 minutes.

sugar sprinkles

One of my favorite cookie trims is a simple sprinkle of plain or colored sugar or edible glitter.

1. Decorate cookies with sugar immediately after rolling and cutting.

2. Don't waste sugar by piling it on too thickly; only the sugar that touches the cookie dough will bake in place.

3. To add texture, score the cookies lightly with a table knife.

Marilyn Cornelius
Test Kitchen Home Economist

Pastry Pillows

If using the food processor to mix the dough, be sure the butter and cream cheese are chilled. If using a mixer, let the butter and cream cheese stand at room temperature 30 minutes to soften.

Prep: 40 minutes **Bake:** 10 to 12 minutes **Chill:** 1 hour **Oven:** 375° **Makes:** 52

2 cups all-purpose flour
¼ teaspoon salt
1 cup butter, cut up
1 8-ounce package cream
   cheese, cut up
   Apricot, peach, raspberry,
   strawberry, or cherry
   preserves
   Almond paste
1 beaten egg
1 tablespoon water
   Coarse or pearl sugar

1 In a food processor bowl* combine flour and salt. Cover and process until mixed. Add butter and cream cheese. Cover and process until combined. (Or, in a medium mixing bowl beat softened butter and cream cheese with an electric mixer until combined. Add flour and salt; beat on low speed of mixer just until combined.)

2 Divide dough in half. Cover and chill the dough at least 1 hour or until it is easy to handle.

3 On lightly floured surface, roll half of the dough at a time to ⅛-inch thickness. Cut dough into 2-inch squares. Place half of the dough squares on an ungreased cookie sheet. Place a scant ¼ teaspoon each of preserves and almond paste in the center of each square.

4 Combine beaten egg and water. Brush edges of layered squares with egg mixture. Top each layered square with a plain dough square. Lightly press edges together; then seal all edges with tines of a fork. Brush filled and sealed dough squares with egg mixture. Sprinkle lightly with coarse or pearl sugar.

5 Bake in a 375° oven for 10 to 12 minutes or until golden. Transfer cookies to a wire rack; cool.

***Note:** If using a small-capacity food processor, mix half of the ingredients at a time.

Nutrition Facts per cookie: 74 cal.,
5 g total fat (3 g sat. fat), 18 mg chol.,
61 mg sodium, 5 g carbo., 0 g fiber,
1 g pro.

Double-Fudge Pockets

If these chocolate-stuffed chocolate cookies fail to satisfy your chocolate craving, drizzle the tops with melted chocolate and forego the powdered sugar sprinkle.

Prep: 35 minutes **Bake:** 10 to 12 minutes **Chill:** 1 hour **Oven:** 350° **Makes:** 30

1 cup butter, softened
1 cup granulated sugar
1 teaspoon baking powder
1 egg
1 egg yolk
1 teaspoon vanilla
½ cup unsweetened cocoa powder
2½ cups all-purpose flour
1 recipe Fudge Filling
   Sifted powdered sugar

1 In a large mixing bowl beat butter with an electric mixer on medium to high speed for 30 seconds. Add granulated sugar and baking powder. Beat until combined, scraping sides of bowl occasionally. Beat in whole egg, egg yolk, and vanilla. Beat in cocoa powder and as much of the flour as you can with the mixer. Using a wooden spoon, stir in any remaining flour.

2 Divide dough in half. Cover and chill the dough for 1 hour or until it is easy to handle.

3 On a lightly floured surface, roll half of the dough at a time to ⅛-inch thickness. Using a floured scalloped 2½-inch cookie cutter, cut out dough. Place half of the cutouts 1 inch apart on an ungreased cookie sheet. Spoon a rounded teaspoon of Fudge Filling into the center of each round. Place another round over the filling. Press edges together to seal.

4 Bake in a 350° oven for 10 to 12 minutes or until edges are firm. Cool on the cookie sheet for 1 minute. Transfer to a wire rack; cool completely. Store cookies in the refrigerator. Before serving, sprinkle with powdered sugar.

Fudge Filling: In a heavy small saucepan melt 4 ounces semisweet chocolate, stirring constantly. Remove from heat. Stir in ½ cup dairy sour cream and ¼ cup finely chopped walnuts. Mixture will stiffen as it cools.

Nutrition Facts per cookie: 160 cal., 9 g total fat (5 g sat. fat), 33 mg chol., 84 mg sodium, 16 g carbo., 1 g fiber, 2 g pro.

To Make Ahead: Bake cookies as directed and cool completely. Place in a freezer container or bag and freeze up to 3 months. Before serving, thaw cookies in the refrigerator.

AlterKNITS

Imaginative Projects AND *Creativity Exercises*

[LEIGH RADFORD]

Photographs by John Rizzo

STC CRAFT | A MELANIE FALICK BOOK

STEWART, TABORI & CHANG
NEW YORK

Published in 2005 by
Stewart, Tabori & Chang
An imprint of Harry N. Abrams, Inc.

Text copyright © 2005 Leigh Radford

All photographs except page 72 © 2005 John Rizzo
Photograph page 72 © 2005 John Mulligan

Editor: Melanie Falick
Designer: goodesign
Production Manager: Kim Tyner

Library of Congress Cataloging-in-Publication Data

Radford, Leigh.
 Alterknits | Leigh Radford ; photographs by John Rizzo.
    p. cm.
 Includes bibliographical references and index.
 ISBN-13: 978-1-58479-455-4
 ISBN-10: 1-58479-455-0
 1. Knitting--Patterns. I. Title.

TT825.R28 2005
746.43'2041--dc22

2004028000

The text of this book was composed in Scala and Futura

Printed and bound in China

10 9 8 7 6 5

HNA
harry n. abrams, inc.
a subsidiary of La Martinière Groupe

115 West 18th Street
New York, NY 10011
www.hnabooks.com

"LET THE BEAUTY we love

BE WHAT we do."

—RUMI

[TABLE *of* CONTENTS]

[INTRODUCTION]

Alter: to make different without changing into something else

KNITTING HAS BEEN A CONSTANT ELEMENT IN MY LIFE EVER SINCE I FIRST LEARNED OVER TWENTY YEARS AGO. WHILE IT HAS AT TIMES TAKEN A BACKSEAT TO OTHER INTERESTS, I CAN'T RECALL EVER NOT HAVING AT LEAST ONE PROJECT ON MY NEEDLES.

THE IDEA FOR ALTERKNITS CAME TO ME A FEW YEARS AGO WHEN I FELT COMPELLED TO INCORPORATE CHANGES INTO MY KNITTING. OVER TIME I HAD DESIGNED AND KNITTED SWEATERS AND OTHER PROJECTS USING A FULL ARRAY OF TRADITIONAL TECHNIQUES AND I felt eager to become more innovative. I BEGAN TO WONDER WHAT ALTERATIONS I COULD MAKE TO TRADITIONAL PATTERNS OR TECHNIQUES IN ORDER TO REORDER THE WAY I—AND OTHERS—LOOKED AT knitting's potential. I DIDN'T WANT TO MAKE MY KNITTING UNRECOGNIZABLE, BUT I WANTED TO PRESENT IT IN A DIFFERENT LIGHT. I USED THE DEFINITION OF "ALTER" (ABOVE) FROM WEBSTER'S NEW COLLEGIATE DICTIONARY AS A GUIDE THROUGHOUT THE CREATIVE PROCESS.

AS I DELVED DEEPER AND DEEPER INTO THE POSSIBILITIES, I BEGAN TO FOCUS MOST ON THE TYPES OF FABRICS THAT COULD BE CREATED WITH KNITTING, just by experimenting with material and needle size. I WORKED WITH EVERYTHING FROM TRADITIONAL YARN TO RIBBON, PAPER, SILVER WIRE, AND CUT-UP FABRIC. I ALSO EXPLORED WAYS OF EMBELLISHING MY KNITTING WITH SUCH TECHNIQUES AS EMBROIDERY, BEADING, CROCHET, AND EVEN FABRIC PAINT, AND ALTERING MY KNITTED FABRIC BY FELTING IT. NOT SURPRISINGLY, AS EACH PROJECT EVOLVED, my sense of the possibilities expanded. SOON I WAS LOOKING AT A DOOR FRAME AND THINKING ABOUT KNITTING A SCREEN (PAGE 106), EYEING A BEAT-UP CHAIR AT A THRIFT SHOP AND DREAMING UP A NEW CUSHION (PAGE 48). EVEN MY DRESS FORM BECAME FAIR GAME. WHY NOT COVER IT WITH ALL OF THOSE PAPER YARN BANDS PILING UP (PAGE 110)? I HEMMED THE NECKLINE AND CUFFS OF A KNITTED RAGLAN SWEATER WITH VELVET (PAGE 40) AND SLIPPED A LENGTH OF SILK CHIFFON INTO A

KNITTED TUBE SCARF (PAGE 18) TO ADD NEW DIMENSIONS IN BOTH COLOR AND TEXTURE. I started to question the accepted wisdom THAT A SWEATER NEED BE SYMMETRICAL, THAT IT OUGHT TO BE KNIT AT ONE GAUGE. I FOUND THAT MY ABILITY TO "ALTER" WAS A MUSCLE THAT, WITH PRACTICE, GOT STRONGER. The process was empowering and exciting.

IN THIS BOOK I SHARE MY PROJECTS WITH YOU. WHILE I, OF COURSE, HOPE YOU WILL MAKE THEM, MORE THAN THAT, I HOPE THEY WILL inspire you to expect the unexpected, TO ENJOY THE REWARDS OF EXPERIMENTATION, AND TO see the possibilities of knitting with broader vision. ON THE INSIDE FRONT COVER OF THIS BOOK IS AN ALTERKNITS NOTEBOOK IN WHICH TO WRITE DOWN NEW IDEAS AND TO WORK ON MANY OF THE AlterExercises I HAVE SCATTERED THROUGHOUT THIS BOOK TO FURTHER INSPIRE YOU. THE BOUNDARIES OF KNITTING MAY NOT BE LIMITLESS, BUT THEY ARE WIDE, AND I AM SURE THAT WE HAVE NOT EVEN COME CLOSE TO MEETING THEM. Start exploring them and let's have fun together!

— LEIGH

PROJECT #01

Silk Skull Caps

• • •

EACH OF THE TWO CAPS PRESENTED HERE IS altered in a different way. SALLY'S CABLES AND LACE (SEE LEFT) IS EMBELLISHED WITH BEADS. ANTOINETTE'S SQUARES (SEE PAGE 13) combines knitting and crochet. THE STITCH PATTERN FOR ANTOINETTE'S SQUARES COMES FROM MON TRICOT 250 PATTERNS TO KNIT AND CROCHET.

SALLY'S CABLES AND LACE
(ANTOINETTE'S SQUARES)

FINISHED MEASUREMENTS
Approximately 20 (22½)" in circumference

YARN
Fiesta La Luz (100% silk; 210 yards / 2 ounces): 1 skein for each cap. Shown in #19 cactus bloom (A); #15 pinon (B).

NEEDLES
One set of 4 or 5 double-pointed needles (dpn) size US 5 (3.75 mm)
Change needle size if necessary to obtain the correct gauge.

NOTIONS
Yarn needle, approximately 100 size 8 seed beads, cable needle (cn), beading needle, crochet hook size D/3 (3.25 mm)

GAUGE
28 sts and 34 rows = 4" in Stockinette stitch (St st)

SPECIAL TERM
C6B: Slip 3 sts to cn, hold to back, k3, k3 from cn.

STITCH PATTERN
LACE CABLE (multiple of 11 sts; 8-rnd repeat)
Rnd 1 and all odd-numbered rnds: Knit.
Rnd 2: * Yo, ssk, k1, k2tog, yo, k6; repeat from * around.
Rnd 4: K1, * yo, slip 1, k2tog, psso, yo, k1, C6B, k1; repeat from * around, ending last repeat C6B.
Rnd 6: * Yo, ssk, yf, slip 1, slipping bead into place, yb, k2tog, yo, k6; rep from * around.
Rnd 8: K1, * yo, slip 1, k2tog, psso, yo, k8; repeat from * around, ending last repeat k7.
Rnd 10: Repeat Rnd 6.
Repeat Rnds 3–10 for Lace Cable

SALLY'S CABLES AND LACE CAP
SET-UP: Using beading needle, thread all beads onto yarn A. CO 121 sts; divide sts evenly onto 3 or 4 needles. Join for working in the rnd, being careful not to twist sts; place marker (pm) for beginning of rnd.

Begin Lace Cable; work Rnds 1–10 once, then repeat Rnds 3–10 until piece measures 4" from the beginning, ending with Rnd 4 of Chart.
Next Rnd: Knit, increasing 4 sts evenly around—125 sts.

SHAPE CROWN: Change to St st.
Rnd 1: * Slip 1, k1, psso, k21, k2tog; repeat from * around—115 sts remain.
Rnd 2: Knit even.

[11]

Rnd 3: * Slip 1, k1, psso, k19, k2tog; repeat from * around—
105 sts remain.

Rnd 4: Knit even.

Continue as established, decreasing 10 sts every other rnd until
15 sts remain, ending after a decrease rnd. Break yarn, leaving
a 12" tail. Using yarn needle threaded with tail, run tail through
remain sts; pull snugly to close opening and fasten off.
Weave in ends.

ANTOINETTE'S SQUARES CAP

Note: For crochet instructions, see Special Techniques, page 115.

MAKE SIX CROCHET SQUARES AS FOLLOWS:

Using crochet hook and B, ch 8, join with a sl st in first ch to form
a ring; do not turn.

Rnd 1: Work 16 sc in ring, join with a sl st in sc at beg of rnd.

Rnd 2: Ch 3, * ch 4, skip 1 sc, work dc in next st; repeat from *
around, ending ch 4, join with a sl st in third ch of beg ch-3.

Rnd 3: Work [1 sc, 1 dc, 2 tr, 1 dc, 1 sc] in each ch-4 space around.

Rnd 4: Ch 3 (counts as dc), work [ch 5, 1 sc between the 2-tr of next
group, ch 5, 1 sc between the 2-tr of next group, ch 5, * 1 dc
between the next 2-sc] 4 times, ending last repeat at *, then sl st in
third ch of beg ch-3.

Rnd 5: Ch 3 (counts as dc), work 2 dc in third ch of ch-3 at beg of
preceding rnd, work [5 dc in each of next 3 ch-5 spaces, 3 dc in next
dc (for corner)] 3 times, end 5 dc in each of the last 3 ch-5 spaces,
join with a sl st in third ch of beg ch-3.

ASSEMBLE SQUARES: With yarn threaded onto yarn needle,
sew squares together, using mattress st or method desired, to form
a ring.

Using dpn and B, pick up and knit 125 sts around top of squares.
Join for working in the rnd; pm for beginning of rnd.

SHAPE CROWN: Work as for Sally's Cables and Lace Cap.

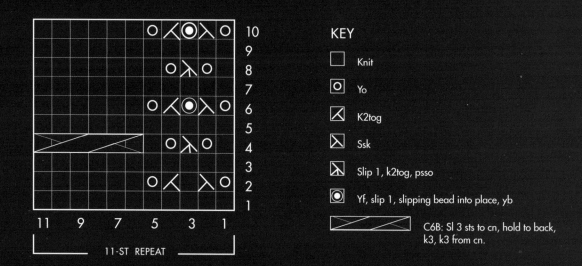

LACE CABLE CHART

KEY

☐ Knit

○ Yo

⊠ K2tog

⊠ Ssk

⊠ Slip 1, k2tog, psso

◉ Yf, slip 1, slipping bead into place, yb

⬚ C6B: Sl 3 sts to cn, hold to back,
k3, k3 from cn.

11-ST REPEAT

"THE REAL voyage of discovery CONSISTS NOT IN SEEKING NEW LANDSCAPES, BUT IN HAVING new eyes."

– MARCEL PROUST

Faux Ruffle Tank

— • —

THIS TANK IS WORKED IN ONE COLOR AND THEN embellished with novelty yarn SEWN INTO THE RIB PANEL TO CREATE THE LOOK OF A RUFFLE. RIBBON ALONE OR A COMBINATION OF RIBBON AND YARN WORK JUST AS WELL FOR THE RUFFLE. Experiment to figure out what you like best.

FINISHED MEASUREMENTS
32 (36, 40, 44)" chest
Shown in size 32"

YARN
S. R. Kertzer Super 10 (100% mercerized cotton; 249 yards / 125 grams): 4 skeins (MC). Shown in #3832 stonewash.

S. R. Kertzer Ranee (80% nylon/20% polyester; 77 yards / 50 grams): 1 skein (CC). Shown in #51 dark blue.

NEEDLES
One set straight needles size US 8 (5 mm)
Change needle size if necessary to obtain the correct gauge.

NOTIONS
Yarn needle, size H/8 (5 mm) crochet hook, stitch markers

GAUGE
20 sts and 28 rows = 4" in Stockinette stitch (St st)
19 sts and 28 rows = 4" in Rib panel

NOTE
To create smooth edges on garment pieces, work edge (selvage) stitches throughout pattern, as follows:
Slip the first st knitwise on every row, and knit the last st.

FRONT
Using MC, CO 75 (85, 95, 105) sts.
Work 2 rows in Garter st.

ESTABLISH PATTERN: Row 1 (RS): Slip 1 (edge st), k24 (29, 34, 39), place marker (pm); * [p1, k2] 8 times, p1; pm, k25 (30, 35, 40).
Row 2: Slip 1 (edge st), purl across to last st, slipping markers, k1.
Repeat Rows 1 and 2, slipping markers every row, until piece measures 13 (13½, 14, 14½)" from the beginning, ending with a WS row.

SHAPE ARMHOLE: (RS) BO 3 (4, 5, 6) sts at the beginning of the next 2 rows—69 (77, 85, 93) sts remain.
(RS) Decrease 1 st each side this row, then every 4 rows 3 (4, 5, 6) times—61 (67, 73, 79) sts remain.
Work even until armhole measures 1½ (2, 2½, 3)" from beginning of shaping, ending with a WS row; pm each side of center 23 sts.

SHAPE NECK: (RS) Work across to marker; join a second ball of yarn and BO center sts for neck; work to end.
Working both sides at same time, at each neck edge, dec 1 st every row 5 (6, 7, 8) times, then every other row 4 times— 10 (12, 14, 16) sts remaining each side for shoulder.
Work even until armhole measures 6½ (7, 7½, 8)".
BO remaining sts.

BACK

Using MC, CO 75 (85, 95, 105) sts. Work 2 rows in Garter st. Begin St st; work even until piece measures 13 (13½, 14, 14½)" from beginning, ending with a WS row.

SHAPE ARMHOLE: As for Front—61 (67, 73, 79) sts remain. Work even until armhole measures 3½ (4, 4½, 5)" from beginning of shaping, ending with a WS row; pm each side of center 31 sts.

SHAPE NECK: (RS) Work across to marker; join a second ball of yarn and BO center sts for neck; work to end. Working both sides at same time, at each neck edge, decrease 1 st every row 5 (6, 7, 8) times— 10 (12, 14, 16) sts remaining each side for shoulder. Work even until armhole measures same as Back to shoulder; BO remaining sts.

FINISHING

Block pieces to measurements.

FAUX RUFFLE: The rib panel worked at center Front has a purl bump every other row in each of the 9 Garter st ribs flanking the St sts. Lay the Front on a flat surface. Thread 2 strands of CC onto yarn needle. Beginning with the first purl bump on one of the ribs, leaving a tail to be woven in later, insert yarn needle from WS to RS through piece into the space between the CO edge and first row of the stitch pattern. Work backstitch loosely up the rib, catching back sts at each purl bump. Continue to the neck edge; pull needle to WS of piece. Tie off. Repeat for the remaining 8 ribs, being careful not to pull too tightly, which may cause the Front to pull up.
Note: You may find it helpful to pin the Front to a towel while creating the ruffles—this will help keep it at the original finished length.

Sew shoulder and side seams. Using crochet hook and MC, work 1 rnd in sc (see Special Techniques, page 115) around neck edge and armholes. Weave in loose ends.

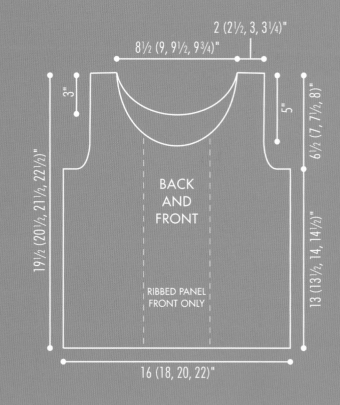

FAUX RUFFLE TANK

2 (2½, 3, 3¼)"

8½ (9, 9½, 9¾)"

3"

5"

6½ (7, 7½, 8)"

19½ (20½, 21½, 22½)"

BACK AND FRONT

RIBBED PANEL FRONT ONLY

13 (13½, 14, 14½)"

16 (18, 20, 22)"

A DREAM KNITTING PARTY

IN YOUR *ALTERKNITS* NOTEBOOK, ANSWER THE FOLLOWING QUESTION:

If you could invite any three people (alive or dead) to hang out
and knit with you, who would you invite and why? Assume they already
know how to knit or would be willing to learn.

HERE'S MY GUEST LIST

Wassily Kandinsky
He is my favorite painter —I'm continually inspired by his use of color,
shape, and composition.

Georgia O'Keeffe
She had such a lovely sensibility for color and scale; it would be fun
to see how she might apply that to her knitting.

Vivienne Westwood
This British fashion designer seems fearless to me. She really mixes
things up—is a bit outrageous—with fabulous results.

Now, make a real list of friends and family with whom you'd like to knit,
then really invite them to your place for a day or evening
of knitting and camaraderie. Ask them to think about who they'd invite to their
dream knitting party and to bring their answers to your get-together.
You'll definitely learn something new about each other.

"THE MOST beautiful THING WE CAN experience IS THE mysterious. IT IS THE SOURCE OF ALL TRUE art and science."
—ALBERT EINSTEIN

Multilayered Tube Scarf and Shawl

THIS PROJECT IS A SIMPLE KNITTED TUBE THROUGH WHICH A LENGTH OF FABRIC IS SLIPPED. The variations are endless BECAUSE YOU CAN EASILY CHANGE THE YARN YOU KNIT WITH AND/OR THE FABRIC WITH WHICH YOU PAIR IT. I love the juxtaposition OF THE fluffy mohair-BLEND YARN AND THE luxurious silk chiffon FABRIC SHOWN HERE.

FINISHED MEASUREMENTS
Scarf: 10" in circumference x 32" long
Shawl: 24" in circumference x 72" long

YARN
Habu Kusakizome (60% mohair, 40% silk; 370 yards /
1 ounce): 1 skein (A). Scarf shown in #32 suo.

Rowan Kid Silk Haze (70% mohair, 30% silk; 229 yards /
25 grams): 3 skeins (B). Shawl shown in #596 marmalade.

NEEDLES
One 16" long circular (circ) needle size US 8 (5 mm)

FABRIC
Silk chiffon: 1 yard, cut to 23" x 36" for Scarf; 2½ yards,
cut to 55" x 90" for Shawl

NOTIONS
Sewing thread to match fabric, beads to embellish ends
of fabric (optional)

GAUGE
19 (18) sts and 23 rows = 4" in Stockinette stitch (St st)
using A (B)
Gauge is not critical for this project.

SCARF AND SHAWL
Using A (B), CO 45 (108) sts. Join for working in the rnd,
being careful not to twist sts; place marker (pm) for
beginning of rnd. Begin St st; work even until piece
measures 32 (72)" from the beginning. BO all sts using
Half-Hitch (sewn) BO method (see Special Techniques,
page 114), or other flexible BO.

FINISHING
Cut fabric to dimensions given at left or desired length.
Note: Fabric should be cut longer than the knitted tube.
Serge ends of fabric, or hand-sew a rolled edge, if desired.
Insert fabric into center of knitted tube (see photo) and
embellish ends with beads, if desired.

"AN ESSENTIAL ASPECT OF CREATIVITY
IS not being afraid to fail."
—DR. EDWIN LAND

PROJECT #04

Modern Bustier

— • —

I LOVE ADDING surprising OR NOT IMMEDIATELY noticeable elements to my designs. FROM THE FRONT, THIS APPEARS TO BE A BASIC TANK. FROM THE BACK (SEE PAGE 23) IT IS A SEXY, SOPHISTICATED CREATION THAT CAN BE DRESSED UP OR DOWN FOR ANY LOOK FROM royal elegance TO perfect punk.

FINISHED MEASUREMENTS

34 (38, 42, 46)" chest; shown in size 34"

YARN

Jaeger Trinity (40% silk, 35% cotton, 25% polymide; 219 yards / 50 grams): 4 (5, 6, 7) skeins. (Use double strand throughout.) Shown in #447 thrift.

NEEDLES

One 29" circular (circ) needle size US 8 (5 mm)
Two double-pointed needles (dpn) size US 8 (5mm)
Change needle size if necessary to obtain the correct gauge.

NOTIONS

Stitch markers, stitch holders, ½ yard silk fabric, sewing thread, sewing needle, 54 approximately ¼" metal eyelets (available at fabric and paper stores), 1 yard cord or ribbon for lacing

GAUGE

17 sts and 28 rows = 4" in Stockinette stitch (St st) using 2 strands yarn held together

STITCH PATTERNS

LEFT BACK BRANCH PANEL (panel of 8 sts; 8-row repeat)
Row 1 (RS): K2, place marker (pm), ssk, k3, yo, k1, pm.
Row 2 and all WS rows: Purl, slipping markers (sm).
Row 3: K2, sm, ssk, k2, yo, k2, sm.
Row 5: K2, sm, ssk, k1, yo, k3, sm.
Row 7: K2, sm, ssk, yo, k4, sm.
Row 8: Repeat Row 2.
Repeat Rows 1–8 for Left Back Branch Panel.

RIGHT BACK BRANCH PANEL (panel of 8 sts; 8-row repeat)
Row 1 (RS): Pm, k1, yo, k3, k2tog, pm, k2.
Row 2 and all WS rows: Purl, slipping markers (sm).
Row 3: Sm, k2, yo, k2, k2tog, sm, k2.
Row 5: Sm, k3, yo, k1, k2tog, sm, k2.
Row 7: Sm, k4, yo, k2tog, sm, k2.
Row 8: Repeat Row 2.
Repeat Rows 1–8 for Right Back Branch Panel.

NOTE

Bustier is worked with 2 strands of yarn throughout.

BUSTIER

Using 2 strands of yarn and long-tail cast-on method (see Special Techniques, page 114), CO 132 (148, 166, 182) sts. Work 2 rows in Garter st, pm after St 32 (36, 40, 44) and St 100 (112, 126, 138) on second row—32 (36, 40, 44) sts each side for left and right Backs; 68 (76, 86, 94) sts for Front.

EYELET EDGING: (WS) P1 * yo, p2tog; rep from * across, ending p1. Purl 2 rows even, ending with a WS row. Begin St st; work even for 2 rows.

SHAPE FRONT

SHORT ROWS (see Special Techniques, page 115):
(RS) Work across 32 (36, 40, 44) sts of left Back, sm; work across 48 (56, 66, 74) sts of Front, wrap next st and turn (wrp-t) as follows: yf, slip 1, yb (stitch wrapped), return wrapped st to left-hand needle—20 sts left unworked—19 sts plus wrapped st, turn.

[21]

(WS) Work across to 20 sts before left side marker, wrp-t as follows: yb, slip 1, yf (stitch wrapped), return wrapped st to left-handle needle, turn.

Working wraps with wrapped sts as you come to them, continue as follows:

(RS) Work to 15 sts before right side marker, wrp-t.

(WS) Work to 15 sts before left side marker, wrp-t.

(RS) Work to 10 sts before right side marker, wrp-t.

(WS) Work to 10 sts before left side marker, wrp-t.

Work 2 rows even in St st.

ESTABLISH PATTERN: (RS) Work Row 1 of Left Back Branch Panel across first 8 sts; in St st, work across to last 8 sts; work Row 1 of Right Back Branch Panel to end. Continuing to work Branch Panels on first and last 8 sts of every row, work even until piece measures 4" from beginning, measured on Back (Front is longer due to Short Rows).

SHAPE WAIST

Row 1: Work across to 16 sts before first marker; * k2tog, k14, sm, k14, ssk *; knit across to 16 sts before second marker; repeat * to *, work as established to end—4 sts decreased; 128 (144, 162, 178) sts remain.

Rows 2, 4, and 6: Work even as established.

Row 3: Work across to 19 sts before first marker; k1-f/b, k3, k2tog, k13, sm, k14, ssk, k2, k1-f/b, knit across to 20 sts before second marker, k1-f/b, k3, k2tog, k14, sm, k13, ssk, k3, k1-f/b, work as established to end.

Row 5: Work across to 15 sts before first marker; k2tog, k13, sm, k14, ssk, knit to 16 sts before second marker, k2tog, k14, sm, k13, ssk, work to end—4 sts decreased; 124 (140, 158, 174) sts remain.

Row 7: Work across to 18 sts before first marker; k1-f/b, k3, k2tog, k12, sm, k14, ssk, k2, k1-f/b, work to 20 sts before second marker, k1-f/b, k3, k2tog, k14, sm, k12, ssk, k3, k1-f/b, work to end.

Work even as established for 2½".

Row 1: Work as established to 15 sts before side marker, k1-f/b, k14, sm, k14, k1-f/b; repeat from * once, work to end—4 sts increased; 128 (144, 162, 178) sts.

Rows 2–4: Work even as established.

Rows 5–16: Repeat Rows 1–4—140 (156, 174, 190) sts.

Work even until Back measures 12¾" or 1" less than desired length, from beginning, ending with a WS row.

Change to St st on all sts; work even for 2 rows.

SHORT ROWS: (RS) Continuing in St st, work across left Back sts, sm; work to 25 sts before right side marker, wrp-t. (WS) Work across to 25 sts before left side marker, wrp-t. Repeat Short Rows, working to 20, 15, 10, then 5 sts before each side marker. (RS) Knit 2 rows (Garter ridge).

SHAPE NECK

(RS) BO 14 (16, 18, 20) sts (one st remaining on needle), work next 4 sts and place 5 sts on holder; BO 30 (34, 38, 42) sts for underarm; repeat * to * for strap; BO 32 (36, 42, 46) sts for center Front; repeat * to * for strap; BO 30 (34, 38, 42) sts for underarm; repeat * to *; BO remaining 14 (16, 18, 20) sts.

STRAPS

Place 5 Strap sts at right Front onto dpn, attach yarn, ready to work a RS row.

Row 1 (RS): Knit.

Row 2: K1, p3, k1.

Repeat Rows 1 and 2 until Strap measures 11 (11, 11½, 12)"; place sts on holder. Repeat for left Strap. Pin straps to Back at holders; adjust length, if necessary, by adding or subtracting rows on straps. Graft Strap sts to sts on Back holders.

FINISHING

Block piece to measurements. Weave in ends.

LEFT FABRIC PANEL: Cut piece of fabric to measure 6" x 14¼"; fold in half lengthwise and sew ¼" seams as shown in diagram at right, leaving opening to turn. Turn fabric RS out and press with an iron, folding under raw edges of opening. Beginning at top of folded edge, position first eyelet ¼" from top and ¾" in from fold. Continue down panel, positioning eyelets ½" apart. Repeat for right fabric panel reversing eyelets.

Fold Bustier at sides, with WS of Back panels facing out. Position fabric so the side with the opening is overlapping the Branch Panels 1¾"; folded edge with eyelets extends 1¼" beyond Back piece of Bustier. Pin, then sew into place. Thread laces through eyelets.

[AlterExercise]

KEEPING TRACK

Do you look through magazines and books and
pick out projects you'd like to knit only
to put those publications aside and then, later on,
forget exactly where the projects
are to be found? An easy way to keep track is to
make a copy of the project photo and
tape the copy into your *AlterKnits* notebook along
with notes on the location of the pattern.

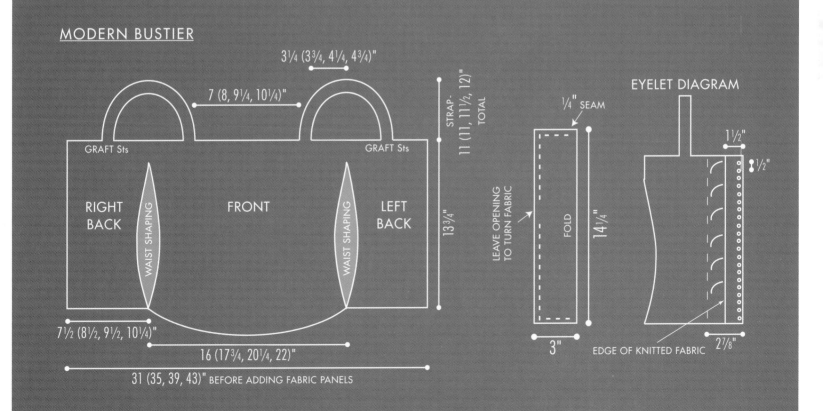

MODERN BUSTIER

3¼ (3¾, 4¼, 4¾)"

7 (8, 9¼, 10¼)"

STRAP- 11 (11, 11½, 12)" TOTAL

GRAFT Sts   GRAFT Sts

RIGHT BACK   WAIST SHAPING   FRONT   WAIST SHAPING   LEFT BACK

13¾"

7½ (8½, 9½, 10¼)"

16 (17¾, 20¼, 22)"

31 (35, 39, 43)" BEFORE ADDING FABRIC PANELS

¼" SEAM

LEAVE OPENING TO TURN FABRIC

FOLD

14¼"

3"

EYELET DIAGRAM

1½"

½"

EDGE OF KNITTED FABRIC

2⅞"

Silver Squares Necklace

THIS ELEGANT NECKLACE IS COMPOSED OF SMALL knitted squares of sterling silver wire and beads SLIPPED ONTO A leather cord. ALL OF THE MATERIALS FOR THIS PROJECT—EXCEPT FOR THE KNITTING NEEDLES—ARE AVAILABLE AT BEAD SHOPS.

FINISHED MEASUREMENTS
Small square: ⁷/₈" x ¾"
Large square: ⁷/₈" x 1"

MATERIALS
1 (30-yard) spool 28-gauge sterling silver wire
(enough for approximately 3 necklaces)
Note: 28-gauge Artistic wire may also be used.

NEEDLES
Two double-pointed needles (dpn) size US 6 (4 mm)
Change needle size if necessary to obtain the correct gauge.

NOTIONS
Stitch holders, 18" or desired length leather cord; leather crimp bead and clasp; 6 spacer beads (Bali Sterling Silver ¼" square—shown); 1 lobster hook; needle-nose pliers; multipurpose cement

GAUGE
30 sts and 32 rows = 4" in Stockinette stitch (St st)

SMALL SQUARE (Make 4)
CO 7 sts; begin St st. Work even for 6 rows; place sts on holder. Weave in loose ends.

LARGE SQUARE (Make 1)
CO 7 sts; begin St st. Work even for 8 rows; finish as for Small Square.

ASSEMBLE NECKLACE
Cut leather cord 18" or desired length.

Dab a small amount of multipurpose cement on end of cord, then slip end into hole at base of crimp bead. Hold firmly in place and pinch crimp bead firmly with pliers.

Lay out beads and knitted squares in order for stringing, alternating spacer beads and knitted wire squares (see photo); place Large Square in the center. Working through the live sts on the knitted squares, string beads and knitted squares onto leather cord.

Attach second half of crimp bead, with lobster hook, to opposite end of leather cord as for first half of crimp bead. Let dry overnight.

Herringbone Leather Cuff

Leather lacing is worked in a woven herringbone stitch FROM BARBARA WALKER'S A TREASURY OF KNITTING PATTERNS TO create this unique cuff. THE LACING, WHILE PLIABLE, DOES TAKE A BIT LONGER TO KNIT THAN MANY TRADITIONAL YARNS. STILL, THIS PROJECT CAN BE completed in about six hours.

FINISHED MEASUREMENTS
2½" wide x 6" in circumference

YARN
1 (100-yard) spool 1mm round leather lacing
(see Sources for Supplies, page 118).

NEEDLES
One set straight needles size US 4 (3.5 mm)
Change needle size if necessary to obtain the correct gauge.

NOTIONS
Yarn needle, crochet hook size E/4 (3.5 mm), bead or button for closure

GAUGE
30 sts and 39 rows = 4" in Stitch Pattern

STITCH PATTERN
WOVEN HERRINGBONE (multiple of 4 sts + 2; 8-row repeat)
Row 1: (RS) K2, * yf, slip 2, yb, k2; rep from * across.
Row 2: P1 * yb, slip 2, yf, p2; rep from * across, end last rep p3.
Row 3: * Yf, slip 2, yb, k2; rep from * to last 2 sts, end yf, sl 2.
Row 4: P3, * yb, slip 2, yf, p2; rep from * across, end last rep p1.
Row 5: * Yf, slip 2, yb, k2; rep from * to last 2 sts, end yf, sl 2.

Row 6: P1, * yb, slip 2, yf, p2; rep from * across, end last rep p3.
Row 7: K2, * yf, slip 2, yb, k2; rep from * across.
Row 8: P3, * yb, slip 2, yf, p2; rep from * across, end last rep p1.

CUFF
CO 18 sts; begin Stitch pattern.
Work Rows 1–4 three times.
Work Rows 5–8 four times.
Work Rows 1–4 four times.
Work Rows 5–8 three times—piece measures 6" from the beginning.
Next Row: (RS) BO all sts in knit.

Place a marker at center of one short side of cuff for button loop. Using crochet hook, work 1 rnd in sc (see Special Techniques, page 115) loosely around edge of cuff, beginning with lower right-hand corner. Work to marker, *ch 5 to create a loop for button, work around to beginning point. Fasten off.

*Note: The exact number of ch sts needed for the loop should be determined by the size of the bead or button you choose to use; you want the loop to slide gently around the bead/button and stay in place.

Crepe Paper Crown

— • —

THE PATTERN BOOK <u>POETRY IN STITCHES</u> BY NORWEGIAN KNITWEAR DESIGNER SOLVEIG HISDAL IS one of my favorites. IN IT THE AUTHOR reveals her creative process BY SHOWING PHOTOS OF HER SOURCES OF INSPIRATION (SUCH AS AN element of nature OR A knitted artifact) AS WELL AS THE GARMENTS THEY INSPIRED. IN ONE SECTION SHE WRITES ABOUT TRADITIONAL NORWEGIAN BRIDES WEARING CROWNS TO THEIR WEDDINGS AND SHOWS A PHOTOGRAPH OF A PAPIER-MÂCHÉ VERSION SHE CREATED. Inspired by these ideas, I decided to knit a crown. I SWATCHED WITH NUMEROUS MATERIALS, INCLUDING CURLY RIBBON AND LONG STRIPS OF ART PAPER, BUT SETTLED ON CREPE PAPER BECAUSE IT IS PLIABLE AND RELATIVELY STRONG. I FOUND THE KEY TO WORKING WITH CREPE PAPER IS TO CAST ON WITH WASTE YARN, THEN KNIT THE PAPER slowly and gently TO AVOID TEARING.

FINISHED MEASUREMENT
Flat 19" long x 3¼" high from bottom of point;
size adjustable at back

CREPE PAPER AND RIBBON
Crepe paper streamers (1¾" wide by 81 feet long):
3 rolls (available where party supplies are sold). Shown
in white and sangria. Six 1-yard lengths and six 1½- yard
lengths decorative fabric ribbon, in varied widths

NEEDLES
One set straight needles size US 10½ (6.5 mm)
Change needle size if necessary to obtain the correct gauge.

NOTIONS
Waste yarn, #8 seed beads, 7 vintage buttons (one for each
crown point), 2 buttons approximately ½" diameter for back
closure, 1 skein embroidery floss to match crepe paper, yarn
needle, sewing needle, beading needle, sewing thread

GAUGE
10 sts and 14 rows = 4" in Stockinette stitch (St st)

CROWN
Using bulky weight waste yarn, CO 49 sts. Unwind crepe
paper from roll, scrunching paper into a thinner strip
(prep about 2–3 yards at a time). Join crepe paper and
begin St st; work even until work measures 2½" from the
beginning.

Next Row: (RS) * Ssk, k3, k2tog; repeat from * across—
35 sts remain; turn.
Next Row: (WS) Purl first 5 sts; place remaining 30 sts
on holder; turn.
* Shape Point: Working on 5 sts only:
Row 1: (RS) Knit.
Rows 2 and 4: Purl.
Row 3: Ssk, k1, k2tog—3 sts remain.
Row 5: Knit.
Row 6: Slip 1 purlwise, p2tog, psso—1 st remains.
Fasten off.

(WS) Purl next 5 sts from holder. Repeat from * 6 times, to create remaining 6 points of Crown.

FINISHING

With warm iron, gently press wrong side of Crown flat. Leave your waste yarn in place or remove and thread ribbon in and out of cast-on stitches to create a decorative bottom border.

EMBELLISHMENTS

Embellish Crown with embroidery stitches, as desired or as follows: Using embroidery floss threaded onto a sewing needle, work random stitches all over the Crown. Using ribbon threaded onto yarn needle, work about 9 double-wrap French knots around Crown.

Embellish with beads and buttons, as desired or as follows:
To create a grouping of beads that lays against the Crown, using beading needle, thread 4 seed beads onto a full strand of embroidery floss (do not divide the floss into separate plies) threaded onto a sewing needle.

Thread needle through knitted fabric of Crown from RS to WS, leaving a 3" tail on the RS. Bring needle back up through knitting to RS next to the place you first inserted the needle; thread the needle back through the beads. Leaving another 3" tail, cut the floss; tie both 3" tails together and trim to ¼" or desired length. Repeat randomly.

To create a grouping of beads in a loop, thread a full strand of embroidery floss onto a sewing needle. Tie a knot at the end of the floss and bring floss up through knitting from WS to RS; thread 4 beads onto the floss; insert needle back through to WS of knitting (creating a loop of beads); tie knot and cut thread. Repeat randomly.

Sew vintage buttons or beads to each Crown point.

CLOSURE

To create an adjustable closure, sew buttons and ribbon to back of Crown (as shown in photo and diagram below). Whipstitch ribbon through back of Crown (along the two vertical rows of stitches on the right and left edges).

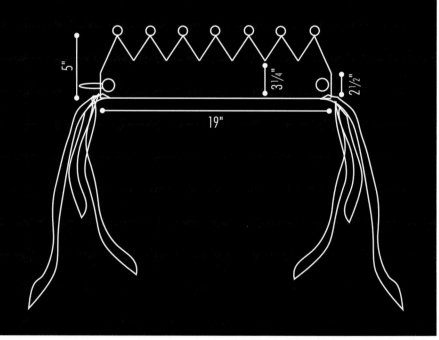

CREPE PAPER CROWN

5"

3¼"

2½"

19"

"THERE IS ONLY one of you IN ALL TIME, THIS expression is unique. AND IF YOU BLOCK IT, IT WILL NEVER EXIST THROUGH ANY OTHER MEDIUM and will be lost."

—MARTHA GRAHAM

Lace-Up Scarf, Shawl, and Wrap

This two-part piece can be worn three different ways. THE 22-INCH-WIDE SHAWL CAN BE WORN ON ITS OWN; THE 7-INCH-WIDE SCARF (SHOWN ON LEFT) CAN BE WORN ON ITS OWN; OR THE TWO PIECES CAN BE laced together with ribbon TO CREATE A MORE VOLUPTUOUS WRAP (SEE PAGE 34). KNITTED WITH A STRAND OF MOHAIR-SILK YARN AND A STRAND OF ALPACA-SILK YARN, THIS IS A fluffy, soft, AND luxurious PIECE.

FINISHED MEASUREMENTS
Shawl: 22" x 78" <Scarf: 7" x 78">

YARN
Rowan Kid Silk Haze (70% mohair, 30% silk; 229 yards / 25 grams): 5 < 2> balls. Shown in #590 pearl (A).
Blue Sky Alpaca's Alpaca and Silk (50% alpaca, 50% silk; 146 yards / 50 grams): 16 < 6 > balls. Shown in #10 ecru (B).

NEEDLES
One set straight needles size US 10 (6 mm)
Change needle size if necessary to obtain the correct gauge.

NOTIONS
Two yarn needles, 4½ yards 2½"-wide silk ribbon, for lacing together scarf and shawl

GAUGE
17 sts and 20 rows = 4" in Fish-Scale Lace using 1 strand of each yarn held together

SPECIAL TERMS
C6B: Slip 3 sts to cn, hold to back, k3, k3 from cn.
C6F: Slip 3 sts to cn, hold to front, k3, k3 from cn.
C8F: Slip 4 sts to cn, hold to front, k4, k4 from cn.

STITCH PATTERNS
VINE LACE (multiple of 9 sts + 4; 4-row repeat)
Row 1 (RS): K3, * yo, k2, ssk, k2tog, k2, yo, k1; rep from * to last st, end k1.
Row 2: Purl.
Row 3: K2, * yo, k2, ssk, k2tog, k2, yo, k1; rep from * to last 2 sts, end k2.
Row 4: Purl.
Repeat Rows 1 – 4 for Vine Lace.

DOWNWARD DOUBLE CABLE (panel of 12 sts; 8-row repeat)
Row 1 (RS): Knit.
Row 2 and all WS rows: Purl.
Row 3: C6F, C6B.
Rows 5 and 7: Knit.
Row 8: Repeat Row 2.
Repeat Rows 1–8 for Cable.

FISH-SCALE LACE (panel of 17 sts; 8-row repeat)
Row 1 (RS): K1, yo, k3, slip 1, k1, psso, p5, k2tog, k3, yo, k1.
Row 2: P6, k5, p6.
Row 3: K2, yo, k3, slip 1, k1, psso, p3, k2tog, k3, yo, k2.
Row 4: P7, k3, p7.
Row 5: K3, yo, k3, slip 1, k1, psso, p1, k2tog, k3, yo, k3.
Row 6: P8, k1, p8.
Row 7: K4, yo, k3, slip 1, k2tog, psso, k3, yo, k4.
Row 8: Purl.
Repeat Rows 1–8 for Fish-Scale Lace.

"IT IS BETTER TO
fail in originality
THAN TO succeed in imitation."

—HERMAN MELVILLE

SCARF STITCH PATTERN (panel of 38 sts; 8-row repeat)
Row 1 (RS): K3, p2, k5, p2, k1, p2, k8, p2, k1, p2, k5, p2, k3.
Row 2 and all WS rows: P3, k2, p5, k2, p1, k2, p8, k2, p1, k2, p5, k2, p3.
Row 3: K3, p2, k2tog, yo, k1, yo, ssk, p2, k1, p2, k8, p2, k1, p2, k2 tog, yo, k1, yo ssk, p2, k3.
Row 5: Repeat Row 1.
Row 7: K3, p2, k2tog, yo, k1, yo, ssk, p2, k1, p2, C8F, p2, k1, p2, k2tog, yo, k1, yo, ssk, p2, k3.
Row 8: Repeat Row 2.
Repeat Rows 1–8 for Scarf St patt.

NOTE
To create smooth edges on garment pieces, work edge (selvage) stitches throughout pattern, as follows: Slip the first st knitwise on every row, and knit the last st.

SHAWL
Using 1 strand of A and 2 strands of B held together, CO 113 sts.

ESTABLISH PATTERN
FOUNDATION ROW: (WS) Slip 1 (edge st), p3, k3, p3, k3, p13, k3, p3, k3, p12, k1, p17, k1, p12, k3, p3, k3, p13, k3, p3, k3, p3, k1 (edge st).

NEXT ROW: (RS) Beginning Row 1 of Stitch Patterns, slip 1 (edge st), k3, p3, k3, p3; work Vine Lace across next 13 sts; p3, k3, p3; work Cable across next 12 sts; p1; work Fish-Scale Lace across next 17 sts; p1; work Cable across next 12 sts; p3, k3, p3; work Vine Lace across next 13 sts; p3, k3, p3, k3, k1 (edge st).

Continue as established until piece measures 78" from the beginning, ending with Row 8 of stitch patterns. BO all sts in pattern.

SCARF
Using 1 strand of A and 2 strands of B held together, CO 38 sts. Begin Scarf St patt; work Rows 3–8 once, then repeat Rows 1–8 even until piece measures 78" from the beginning, ending with Row 3 of Scarf St patt. BO all sts in pattern.

COMBINING SHAWL AND SCARF
Lay both pieces on a flat surface, side by side.

LACES: With both ends of ribbon threaded onto yarn needles, lace through slip stitches at each side of Shawl and Scarf, as though you are lacing shoes, threading ribbon through every 4th row, crossing from one side to the other (see right).

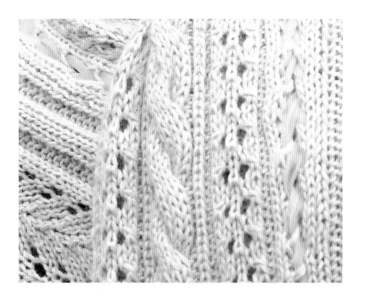

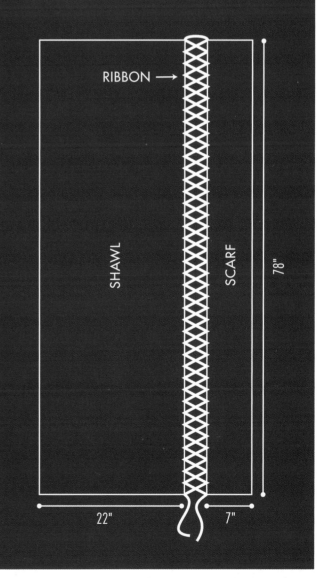

SCARF/SHAWL/WRAP ASSEMBLY

RIBBON →

SHAWL

SCARF

78"

22"

7"

Lace-Up Fingerless Gloves

— • —

I HAVE LOST COUNT OF HOW MANY PAIRS OF FINGERLESS GLOVES I OWN, OR HAVE KNITTED FOR OTHERS. Getting bored with the patterns I had used before, I DECIDED TO DRESS THESE UP BY ADDING LENGTH TO THE CUFF AND THEN lacing it up with silk ribbon.

FINISHED MEASUREMENTS
7½ (8, 8½)" hand circumference
To fit: Woman's Small (Medium, Large)
Shown in size 7½".

YARN AND RIBBON
Manos del Uruguay (100% wool; 138 yards / 100 grams):
1 (1, 2) skeins. Shown in #32 gasoline.

2 yards Hannah Silk bias-cut 1"-wide silk ribbon (cut into two 36-inch pieces). Shown in French toast.

NEEDLES
One set straight needles size US 8 (5mm)
One set of 5 double-pointed needles (dpn) size US 8 (5mm)
Change needle size if necessary to obtain the correct gauge.

NOTIONS
Yarn needle, stitch markers, stitch holder or waste yarn

GAUGE
18 sts and 27 rows = 4" in Stockinette stitch (St st)

GLOVE
Using straight needles, CO 38 (42, 44) sts. Knit 1 row.

ESTABLISH EYELET PATTERN: Working in St st, work eyelets at side edges as follows:
Row 1 (RS): K1, yo, k2tog, knit across to last 3 sts, k2tog, yo, k1.
Rows 2, 4 and 6: P1, k2, purl across to last 3 sts, k2, p1.
Rows 3 and 5: Knit.
Repeat Rows 1 – 6 three times—piece measures 3½".

SHAPE ARM:
Row 1: (RS) K1, yo, (k2tog) twice, knit across to last 5 sts, (k2tog) twice, yo, k1—36 (40, 42) sts remain.
Rows 2 and 4: (WS) P1, k2, purl across to last 3 sts, k2, p1.
Row 3 and 5: Knit.
Row 6: Repeat Row 2.
Repeat Rows 1–6 for arm shaping twice, then work Row 1 of Eyelet Pattern once more—32 (36, 38) sts.
Change to dpn, dividing sts evenly on 4 needles.
Join for working in the rnd. Continuing in St st, work even for 4 rounds.; place marker (pm) for beginning of rnd.

THUMB GUSSET: K15 (17, 18), pm; M1-L, k1, M1-R (see Special Techniques, page 114); pm, knit rem 16 (18, 19) sts — 34 (38, 40) sts. Work even for 2 rnds.
Continuing as established, increase 2 sts inside markers every 3 rnds 4 (4, 5) times—11 (11, 13) Gusset sts inside markers—42 (46, 50) sts. Work 1 rnd even.

HAND: Place Gusset sts on holder or waste yarn, removing markers; CO 1 st over gap for thumb gusset, knit to end— 32 (36, 38) sts remain.

LOWER EDGE HAND
Choose to create either a rolled or ribbed edge (ribbed edge shown).

FOR ROLLED EDGE: Work even for 2½ (2¾, 3)" or desired length. Purl 1 rnd. BO all sts loosely.

FOR RIBBED EDGE: Work even for 1½ (1¾, 2)" or desired length, increasing 0 (0, 2) sts evenly on last rnd—32 (36, 40) sts. Begin k3, p1 rib; work even for 1". BO all sts loosely in pattern.

THUMB: Place sts from holder/waste yarn onto 3 dpn, dividing evenly. Join for working in the rnd; pm for beginning of rnd. Begin St st. First Rnd: Pick up 1 from CO stitch, work to end— 12 (12, 14) sts. Work even for ½ (¾, 1)", or desired length.

LOWER EDGE THUMB
Choose to create either a rolled or ribbed edge (ribbed edge shown).

FOR ROLLED EDGE: Work even for an additional 1". Purl 1 rnd. BO all sts loosely.

FOR RIBBED EDGE: Work even for an additional ½", decreasing 0 (0, 2) sts evenly on last rnd—12 (12, 12) sts remain. Work k3, p1 rib for ½". BO all sts loosely in pattern.

FINISHING
Weave in loose ends, closing up gaps at base of thumb. Thread ribbon through eyelets on cuff as though you are lacing shoes (see photo).

Make second glove to match first.

[AlterExercise]
GRAB BAG

This exercise can be done on your own, but is often more fun in a group.
It is meant to encourage exploration of new and different combinations of yarn,
needle size, and stitch pattern.

TO GET READY
Put a collection of different-sized knitting needles in a paper bag
(at least two needles for each participant; for example, if four people are doing
the exercise, put at least eight needles in the bag).

Put a collection of different types of yarn in a second paper bag (at least one ball
of yarn for each participant; for example, if four people are doing
the exercise, put at least four balls of yarn in the bag). Be sure to include yarns
of different fibers, weights, and textures.

Write instructions for different stitch patterns on index cards (at least one stitch pattern for
each participant). Be sure to choose stitch patterns that all of the participants are
capable of working without too much difficulty. Refer to your favorite stitch dictionary for ideas.

TO START
Ask each participant to close his or her eyes and pick two needles (they don't
need to be the same size), one yarn, and one stitch pattern from the bags, and then,
with eyes opened, knit a swatch accordingly.

TO INCREASE THE LEVEL OF EXPERIMENTATION
Instead of, or in addition to, traditional knitting yarns, place alternative types
of yarn in the bag. By alternative yarns, I mean any type of continuous
length of a material not traditionally used for knitting, such as crepe paper, kitchen string,
raffia, or wire. You may even want to try knitting with tape pulled
from an old audio- or videocassette.

Velvet-Trimmed Raglan Pullover

THIS ELEGANT RAGLAN COMBINES comfort with luxury and style. FOR EXTRA FEMININITY, IT INCLUDES GENTLE WAIST SHAPING, a keyhole opening AT THE BACK NECK, AND A velvet finish AT THE NECK AND SLEEVE EDGES. FOR THOSE WHO PREFER TO SKIP THE VELVET EDGING, THE PATTERN INCLUDES TWO OPTIONS: AN ATTACHED I-CORD EDGE AND A CROCHETED EDGE.

FINISHED MEASUREMENTS
32¾ (35¾, 38¾)" chest
Shown in size 35¾"

YARN
GGH Tajmahal (70% merino superfine wool, 22% silk, 8% cashmere; 93 yards / 25 grams): 14 (16, 18) balls. Shown in color #14.

NEEDLES
One 29" circular (circ) needle size US 4 (3.25mm)
One set of 4 or 5 double-pointed needles (dpn) size US 4 (3.25 mm)
Change needle size if necessary to obtain the correct gauge.

NOTIONS
Yarn needle, stitch holders, stitch markers, 1½ yards ⅝"-wide velvet ribbon, sewing needle and thread to match ribbon
Optional: Crochet hook size D/3 (3.25 mm) for crocheted edging

GAUGE
28 sts and 37 rows/rnds = 4" in Stockinette stitch (St st)

SLEEVE (make 2)
Using dpn, CO 58 (62, 66) sts. Join for working in the rnd, being careful not to twist sts; place marker (pm) for beginning of rnd. (WS) Begin St st; work even for 7 rnds.

SHAPE SLEEVE: Increase 1 st each side of marker this rnd, then every 8 rnds 11 times as follows: K1 (seam st), k1-f/b, work around to 1 st before marker, k1-f/b— 82 (86, 90) sts.

Work even until piece measures 17½ (18, 18½)" from beg, ending 6 (7, 8) sts before marker on last rnd. Place next 13 (15, 17) sts on holder for underarm; place remaining 69 (71, 73) sts on a separate holder or waste yarn.

BODY

Using circ needle, CO 226 (246, 262) sts. Join for working in the rnd, being careful not to twist sts; pm for beginning of rnd. (WS) Begin St st; work even until piece measures 2½" from the beginning, pm after first st and 114th (124th, 132nd) st for seam sts.

SHAPE WAIST: Decrease Rnd: * K1 (seam st), sm, ssk, knit to 3 sts before next seam st marker, k2tog: repeat from * once—4 sts decreased; 1 each side of both marked seam sts. Work 6 rounds even. Repeat last 7 rnds 3 times more, then repeat Decrease Rnd once more—206 (226, 242) sts remain. Work even for 1½".

Increase Rnd: K1 (seam st), sm, k1-f/b, work to 2 sts before next marker, k1-f/b, k1, sm, k1-f/b work to 1 st before next marker, k1-f/b—4 sts increased. Work 6 rounds even. Repeat last 7 rnds 4 times more, then work Increase Rnd once more— 230 (250, 266 sts). Work even until piece measures 14" from the beginning, ending 6 (7, 8) sts before beginning of rnd marker on last rnd.

Place seam st and the 6 (7, 8) sts on either side of both seam sts on holders for underarm—13 (15, 17) sts each holder. Place remaining 102 (110, 116) sts each for Front and Back on holders or waste yarn and set aside.

YOKE

Beginning with left Sleeve, k1, pm, knit remaining 68 (70, 72) Sleeve sts, pm; k1 (left Front), pm, knit remaining 101 (109, 115) Front sts, pm; k1 (right Sleeve), pm, knit remaining 68 (70, 72) Sleeve sts, pm; k1 (Back), pm, knit rem 101 (109,115) Back sts— 342 (362, 378) sts—4 seam sts, 101 (109, 115) st each for Front and Back, and 68 (70, 72) sts each Sleeve.
Continuing in St st, work 1 rnd even.

SHAPE RAGLAN: Decrease 8 sts every 4 rnds 10 (11, 12) times as follows:
Decrease Rnd: *K1 (seam st), sm, ssk, work to 2 sts before next marker, k2tog, sm; rep from * 3 times—8 sts decreased.
Work 3 rnds even.
And AT THE SAME TIME, when piece measures 3¼ (3½, 3¾)" from beg of raglan shaping, end with a Decrease Rnd. Work 1 rnd, placing a marker each side of center Back st.

SHAPE BACK KEYHOLE OPENING: Work as established to center Back st, knit center st, turn; p2tog, turn, removing center Back markers; continue as established, ending with second half of Back (work to [p2tog and turn] from beg of row)—1 st decreased on Back. Begin working back and forth in rows for remainder of Yoke, completing shaping as established—261 (273, 281) sts remain.

CONTINUE RAGLAN SHAPING: Work Raglan Decrease row (decreasing 8 sts as established). Work 1 row even. Work last 2 rows 10 (11, 12) times total—181 (185, 185) sts remain; pm each side of center Front 24 (28, 28) sts.

SHAPE FRONT NECK AND CONTINUE RAGLAN SHAPING: (RS) Work Raglan Decrease row, and AT THE SAME TIME, work across to marker for center Front sts; join a second ball of yarn and BO center Front sts for neck, removing center Front markers; work to end, completing Raglan shaping—150 (150, 150) sts remain.

Working both sides at same time, working back and forth in rows, work Raglan Decrease row as established every RS row; and AT THE SAME TIME, at each neck edge, BO 3 sts once and then 2 sts once—124 (124, 124) sts remain. Work Raglan Decrease rows once more—116 (116, 116) sts remain. BO remaining sts.

FINISHING

With threaded yarn needle, sew underarm seams. Weave in loose ends. Choose to create either a velvet, attached I-cord, or crochet edging (velvet shown).

FOR VELVET EDGING

KEYHOLE: Cut ribbon to fit keyhole opening at center Back. With RS facing, beginning at right keyhole opening, fold ribbon in half over knitted edge. Pin into position. With threaded needle, sew into place with a backstitch.

NECKLINE: Beginning at left keyhole edge, attach ribbon as for keyhole, folding raw edges at each end of ribbon under at keyhole openings.

SLEEVES: Cut ribbon to circumference of sleeve plus ½" for seam allowance. With RS's of ribbon together, sew ¼" seam, using straight stitch. Press seam open. Fold ribbon in half and attach as above, lining up ribbon seam and underside of Sleeve.

FOR ATTACHED I-CORD EDGING

Using a dpn, CO 3 sts. * With WS facing, beginning at left Back neck raglan seam, k2, slip 1, pick up and knit 1 st from neck edge, psso, slide sts to right-hand end of needle; repeat from * along Back left neckline to corner of Keyhole.

TURN CORNER: At beginning of keyhole opening, k3, do not pick up a stitch along neck edge; slide sts to right-hand end of needle, k2, slip 1, pick up and knit 1 stitch from corner, psso; slide sts to right-hand end of needle, k3, do not pick up st along neck edge—3 rows of I-cord worked; corner stitch joined.

KEYHOLE: Work attached I-cord around opening, stopping 3 rows before right Back corner; turn corner as for left Back corner. Work attached I-cord along right Back neck and Front neckline to beginning point; BO sts. Sew ends of I-cord tog. Weave in loose ends.

FOR CROCHETED EDGING

Note: For crochet instructions, see Special Techniques, page 115.
With RS facing, beginning at right Back neck raglan seam, work 1 row sc along Back neck to corner of keyhole opening; work 2 sc in corner stitch; work sc around keyhole, working corner as before; continue sc around remainder of neck edge; join to beginning sc with a slip stitch; fasten off.

BUTTON LOOP (for velvet and crocheted edges)
Using yarn needle threaded with yarn, make a small loop at left Back for button. Sew button opposite loop.

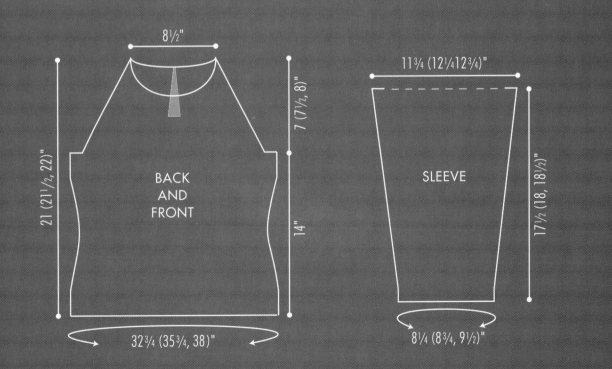

RAGLAN PULLOVER

BACK AND FRONT

8½"

7 (7½, 8)"

21 (21½, 22)"

14"

32¾ (35¾, 38)"

SLEEVE

11¾ (12¼ 12¾)"

17½ (18, 18½)"

8¼ (8¾, 9½)"

"THE WORLD OF reality has its limits;
THE WORLD OF
imagination is boundless."

—JEAN-JACQUES ROUSSEAU

Mohair Cables Pullover

THIS FLUFFY MOHAIR PULLOVER, EASY TO DRESS UP OR DOWN, IS accented with silk ribbon AT THE NECK AND SLEEVES AND a row of tiny buttons UP THE SLEEVES. A SIMPLE CABLE PATTERN, FLANKED BY REVERSE STOCKINETTE STITCH, IS REPEATED ON THE FRONT AND BACK. The natural halo of the mohair shimmers when reflected by the light.

FINISHED MEASUREMENTS
34 (38, 42, 46)" chest
Shown in size size 34"

YARN AND RIBBON
Classic Elite La Gran Mohair (76.5% mohair, 17.5% wool, 6% nylon; 90 yards / 42 grams): 9 (11, 12, 13) balls. Shown in #6518 Vanessa's blue; also shown with Unisex Deconstructed Pullover on page 92 in #6560 coleus.

3 yards Hannah Silk bias-cut 3/8"-wide silk ribbon. Shown in moon goddess.

NEEDLES
One set straight needles size US 9 (5.5 mm)
Change needle size if necessary to obtain the correct gauge.

NOTIONS
Stitch markers, yarn needle, cable needle, crochet hook size I/9 (5.5 mm), twelve 3/8" buttons

GAUGE
14 sts and 20 rows = 4" in Stockinette stitch (St st)

BACK
CO 84 (90, 96, 104) sts.

ESTABLISH PATTERN: (RS) P8 (11, 14, 18) sts (work in Rev St st throughout); place marker (pm) beginning Row 1 of Charts, work 68 center sts as follows: 16 sts Chart A, pm; 10 sts Chart B, pm; 16 sts Chart A, pm; 10 sts Chart C, pm; 16 sts Chart A, pm; p8 (11, 14, 18) sts (work in Rev St st throughout).

Continuing as established, work even until piece measures approximately 21 (22, 23, 24)" from the beginning, ending with Row 4 of Charts. BO all sts in pattern; pm each side of center 32 sts for neck; 26 (29, 32, 36) sts each side for shoulders.

FRONT
Work as for Back until piece measures 19½ (20½, 21½, 22½)" from the beginning (8 rows less than Back to shoulder); pm each side of center 32 sts.

SHAPE NECK: (RS) Work across to marker; join a second ball of yarn and BO center 32 sts; work to end as established. Work even until piece measures same as Back to shoulder, ending with Row 4 of Charts. BO all sts in pattern.

SLEEVE (Make 2)
CO 35 sts; begin Garter st. Work even for 4 rows, ending with
a WS row. (RS) Change to Rev St st; work even for 6 rows, ending
with a WS row.

SHAPE SLEEVE: (RS) Increase 1 st each side this row, then every
6 rows 12 (12, 13, 13) times—61 (61, 63, 63) sts. Work even until
piece measures 19" from the beginning. BO all sts.

FINISHING
Sew shoulder seams. Measure down from shoulder, Back, and
Front 8½ (8½, 9, 9)" and pm; sew sleeves between markers.
Sew side seams; sew sleeve seams, leaving 8½" open at lower edge.
Weave in ends.

PREPARE RIBBON: Cut ribbon into pieces at bias seams and knot
back together, leaving approximately 1½" tails.

NECK EDGING: With RS facing, using crochet hook and ribbon,
work 1 row in sc around neck edge (see Special Techniques,
page 115), pulling knots forward, if desired (see photo).

SLEEVE EDGING: Using crochet hook and ribbon, beginning at
seam, working down right side of Sleeve slit, work button loops as
follows: * Work 1 sc in next 3 sts, ch 1 (for button loop); repeat
from * to lower edge, working a total of 6 button loops; continue in
sc along lower edge of Sleeve and up opposite edge of slit to seam;
fasten off. Repeat for second Sleeve.

Sew buttons opposite button loops.

MOHAIR CABLES PULLOVER

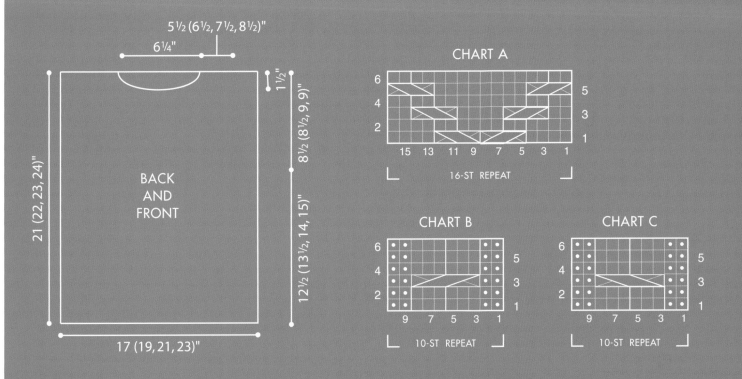

CHART A
16-ST REPEAT

CHART B
10-ST REPEAT

CHART C
10-ST REPEAT

5½ (6½, 7½, 8½)"
6¼"
1½"
8½ (8½, 9, 9)"
12½ (13½, 14, 15)"

21 (22, 23, 24)"

BACK
AND
FRONT

17 (19, 21, 23)"

17¼ (17¼, 18, 18)"

SLEEVE

19"

10"

KEY

☐ Knit on RS, purl on WS

⊡ Purl on RS, knit on WS

C4B: Sl 2 sts to cn, hold to back, k2, k2 from cn.

C4F: Sl 2 sts to cn, hold to front, k2, k2 from cn.

C6B: Sl 3 sts to cn, hold to back, k3, k3 from cn.

C6F: Sl 3 sts to cn, hold to front, k3, k3 from cn.

Custom Cushion

— • —

I love exploring thrift stores and flea markets. WHEN I SCORED THIS LEATHER CHAIR, I IMMEDIATELY STARTED THINKING ABOUT KNITTING A NEW CUSHION FOR IT. I KNEW I WOULD ENJOY the marriage of the worn leather and the soft, shiny, kettle-dyed wool. THE ORIGINAL CUSHION WAS PRETTY BEAT-UP AND PRACTICALLY FLAT, BUT BEFORE TOSSING IT IN THE TRASH, I MEASURED IT CAREFULLY SO I COULD HAVE A NEW PIECE OF FOAM CUT TO THE EXACT DIMENSIONS I NEEDED. WHEN KNITTING THE BACK AND SIDE PANELS, FOLLOW THE COLOR SEQUENCE GIVEN, OR choose your own BY PLANNING IT OUT CAREFULLY IN YOUR ALTERKNITS NOTEBOOK OR BY THROWING ALL OF THE YARN IN A PILE AND PICKING EACH COLOR RANDOMLY (letting serendipity be your guide). MOST UPHOLSTERY SHOPS CAN CUT FOAM FOR YOU OR AT LEAST REFER YOU TO ANOTHER RESOURCE. IF YOU DON'T HAVE A CHAIR THAT NEEDS A CUSHION, CONSIDER MAKING THIS ONE TO BE USED ON THE FLOOR.

FINISHED MEASUREMENTS
20" x 24" x 4" deep

YARN
Manos del Uruguay (100% wool; 138 yards / 100 grams):
6 skeins #G coffee (A), 2 skeins #68 citric (B), 2 skeins brick (E), 2 skeins #M bing cherry (D), 1 skein kohl (C)

NEEDLES
One set straight needles size US 10 (6 mm)
Change needle size if necessary to obtain the correct gauge.

MATERIALS
Recycled chair

NOTIONS
18" zipper, 20" x 24" x 4" piece foam
Note: I took the foam to an upholstery shop—they wrapped the foam with a couple layers of cotton batting and then sewed a cotton twill case for it.

GAUGE
16 sts and 21 rows = 4" in Stockinette stitch (St st)

TOP PANEL
Using A, CO 71 sts. Beginning with Row 1, work Rows 1–110 of Chart. BO all sts in purl.
Finished piece should measure 18½" wide x 22" long.

BOTTOM PANEL

COLOR SEQUENCE: In St st, work 5 rows B, 2E, 4D, 3A, 2C, 2B, 4E, 5A, 7B, 3D, 3E, 2B, 3C, 2A, 10D, 4B, 6A, 3D, 2C, 3B, 8E, 5D, 3C, 8B, 1A.

Using B, CO 71 sts. Knit 2 rows. Begin St st and color sequence; work even until piece measures 22" from the beginning, ending with a RS row. Knit 2 rows. (WS) BO all sts in purl.

SIDE PANEL

COLOR SEQUENCE: In St st, work 13 rows D, 12E, 11B, 5D, 11C, 12D, 6E, 12B, 7C, 7D, 13E, 8C, 2B, 2D, 2C, 2E, 3B, 9D, 11B, 8C, 8E, 16D, 5B, 5C, 5E, 5D, 5C, 8B, 14E, 12D, 6C, 10B, 14E, 4D, 8B, 10C, 3D, 3B, 3C, 3E, 8D, 6C, 9E, 5D, 1B, 2C, 10B, 7D, 10E, 3C, 3B, 3D, 3E, 14C, 13D, 13B, 3C, 4E, 12C.

Using D, CO 15 sts. Begin St st and color sequence; work even until piece measures 87" from the beginning. BO all sts.

FINISHING

EDGING—TOP AND BOTTOM PANELS: With RS facing, using A, pick up and knit 96 sts along the right and left sides (longer edges) of both panels; knit 2 rows. BO all sts.

SIDE PANEL: With RS's together, graft CO edge and BO edge together forming a circle.

JOIN PANELS: Beginning at center Back of the Top Panel, sew Top Panel to Side Panel using mattress st or desired seaming method. Repeat for Bottom Panel, leaving an 18" opening for zipper between the Side Panel and the Bottom Panel at center Back.

INSERT ZIPPER: With the RS of the zipper facing the WS of the panels, pin the zipper into the opening, leaving a ¼" overlap, then stitch zipper into place.

CUSTOM CUSHION COLOR CHART

COLOR KEY:
Knit on RS, purl on WS,
except as noted.

- ▨ A (coffee)
- • A–Knit on WS
- ▨ B (citric)
- ▨ C (kohl)
- ▨ D (bing cherry)

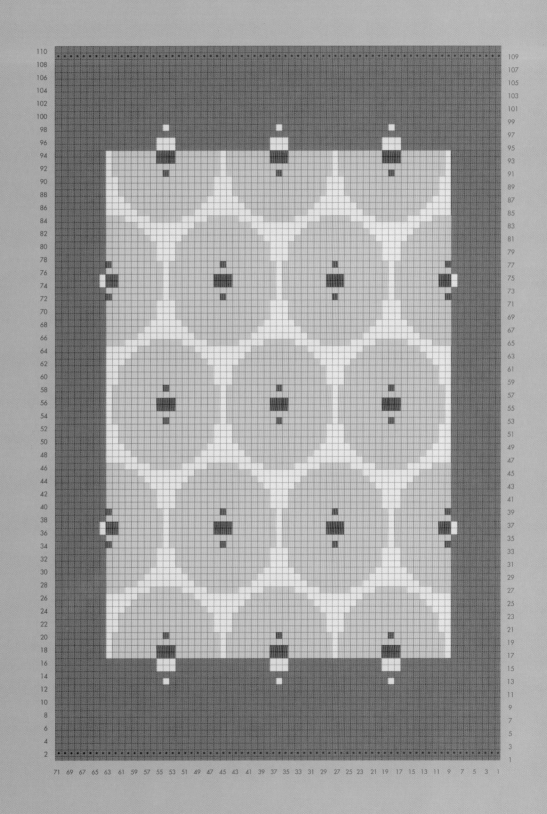

Zigzag Sweater Blanket

THIS REVERSIBLE BLANKET IS CREATED OUT OF sweaters collected from local thrift stores. THE SWEATERS ARE FELTED, CUT INTO "PATCHES," AND SEWN TOGETHER ON A MACHINE USING THE ZIGZAG STITCH. To preserve some of the integrity of the original sweaters, I MADE SURE SOME OF THE ELEMENTS, SUCH AS CUFFS AND COLLARS, REMAINED RECOGNIZABLE ALONG THE PERIMETER OF THE BLANKET. THIS CREATED SOME "irregularities" ALONG THE EDGE, which I love. OF COURSE, IF YOU PREFER A MORE "PERFECT" EDGE, YOU CAN ARRANGE YOUR BLANKET SO THE EDGE IS STRAIGHT.

FINISHED MEASUREMENTS
Approximately 57" x 60"

MATERIALS
8 to 10 adult Large and X-Large sweaters (100% wool—NOT machine-washable),

NOTIONS
Sewing machine, upholstery or top-stitching thread, scissors or rotary cutter, acrylic quilting ruler, iron

FELTING AND PREPARING SWEATERS
Felt the sweaters following the instructions on page 113, noting additional instructions below:
Once sweater is felted sufficiently, if it is machine-knitted, let it run through the spin cycle, then lay flat to dry or put in dryer. If the sweater is handknitted, do not run it through the spin cycle or put it in the dryer. Lay it flat to dry.

BLANKET
Cut felted sweaters apart into dimensions given on diagram on page 54, or desired size, using scissors or quilting ruler and rotary cutter. If felted pieces are not flat, steam-iron them.

On your sewing machine, set your stitch length to 4, and stitch width to the widest possible setting.

Butt raw edges of fabric together with no space in between, lining up fabric-joins with the center of the pressure foot. Sew pieces together using a zigzag stitch. Following diagram, assemble sections as shown, steam-presssing "seams" of fabric-joins flat as you go. Continue piecing together until blanket reaches desired size.

ZIGZAG SWEATER BLANKET

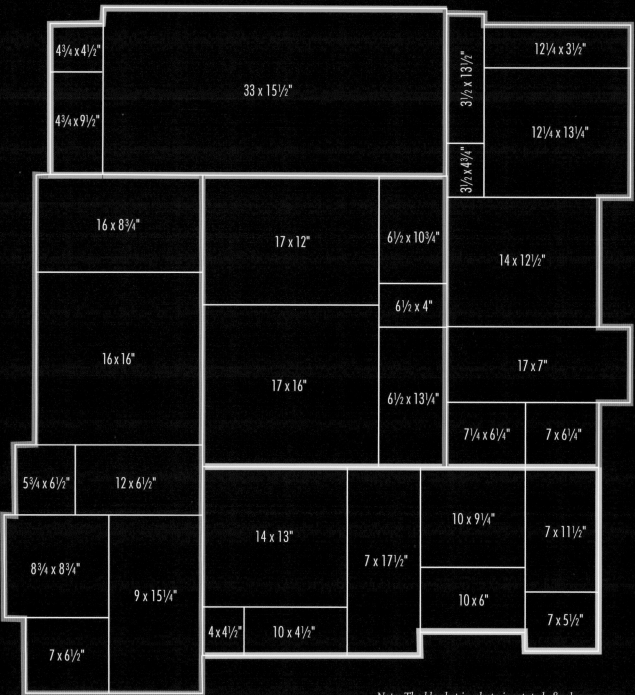

4³⁄₄ x 4¹⁄₂"

4³⁄₄ x 9¹⁄₂"

33 x 15¹⁄₂"

3¹⁄₂ x 13¹⁄₂"

3¹⁄₂ x 4³⁄₄"

12¹⁄₄ x 3¹⁄₂"

12¹⁄₄ x 13¹⁄₄"

16 x 8³⁄₄"

17 x 12"

6¹⁄₂ x 10³⁄₄"

14 x 12¹⁄₂"

16 x 16"

6¹⁄₂ x 4"

17 x 16"

6¹⁄₂ x 13¹⁄₄"

17 x 7"

7¹⁄₄ x 6¹⁄₄"

7 x 6¹⁄₄"

5³⁄₄ x 6¹⁄₂"

12 x 6¹⁄₂"

8³⁄₄ x 8³⁄₄"

9 x 15¹⁄₄"

14 x 13"

7 x 17¹⁄₂"

10 x 9¹⁄₄"

7 x 11¹⁄₂"

10 x 6"

7 x 6¹⁄₂"

4 x 4¹⁄₂"

10 x 4¹⁄₂"

7 x 5¹⁄₂"

Note: The blanket in photo is rotated 180 degrees.

"THE creative thinker IS FLEXIBLE AND ADAPTABLE AND PREPARED TO rearrange his thinking."

—A. J. CROPLEY

Felted Bulletin Board

·—•—·

I HANG BULLETIN BOARDS ALL OVER THE WALLS OF MY STUDIO SO I CAN post sketches, color palettes, and inspirational images and words ON THEM. RATHER THAN EDITING THE POSTINGS ON EXISTING BOARDS WHEN I RUN OUT OF SPACE, I PREFER TO ADD MORE BOARDS. ONE DAY, tired of the traditional cork bulletin BOARDS OFFERED AT OFFICE SUPPLY STORES, I DECIDED TO make a felted version AND SUSPEND IT FROM A BAMBOO POLE. TO KEEP POSTINGS IN PLACE, I USE ORDINARY STRAIGHT PINS OR T-PINS. THUMBTACKS WILL WORK BUT AREN'T AS SECURE. IF YOU DON'T WANT TO PREPARE THE BAMBOO POLE AS GIVEN IN THIS PATTERN, SUBSTITUTE ANY OTHER TYPE OF POLE THAT WILL FIT THROUGH THE RIBBON LOOPS.

FINISHED MEASUREMENTS
30" x 60" before felting; 23¼" x 40½" after felting

YARN
Brown Sheep Lamb's Pride Bulky (85% wool, 15% mohair;
125 yards / 4 ounces): 3 skeins each in 3 colors and 1 skein
in border color (D). Shown in #M89 roasted coffee (A),
#M125 garnet (B), #M145 spice (C), #M42 twilight green (D).

NEEDLES
One 40" circular (circ) needle size US 10½ (6.5 mm)
Two double-pointed needles (dpn) size US 9 (5.5 mm)
Change needle size if necessary to obtain the correct gauge.

NOTIONS
1½ yards ½"-wide fabric ribbon, 5 buttons (optional), thread,
4" diameter bamboo pole, cut to 46½" or desired length,
heavy-gauge sandpaper, fine-gauge sandpaper, small can
mahogany wood stain

GAUGE
14 sts and 20 rows = 4" in Stockinette stitch (St st),
using circ needle, before felting

BULLETIN BOARD
Using circ needle, CO 100 sts; begin St st. Work three
sections, each 19¾" long, using A, B, then C—piece
measures approximately 60" in total length. BO all sts.
Weave in loose ends.

BORDER: Using dpn and D, CO 4 sts; begin I-cord
(see Special Techniques, page 114). Knit 4, do not turn.

Work attached I-cord around Bulletin Board as follows:
* Slide sts to the right, k3, slip 1, with WS of piece facing,
pick up and knit 1 st from edge of Bulletin Board, psso.
Repeat from * until entire perimeter is worked. Join ends,
fasten off.

FELTING AND BLOCKING
Felt the Bulletin Board following instructions on page 113.

Block the felted Bulletin Board to ensure it remains flat and
maintains the desired shape by pinning it while wet to the
desired dimensions and leaving it undisturbed until it is
completely dry.

FINISHING

Cut ribbon into 5 pieces, each measuring 10⅝"
in length. With RS's together, sew ends together
using a ⅝" seam. Turn so that the WS's are facing
each other and press seam flat. Sew into place,
evenly spaced along top of Board; sew on buttons
for embellishment, if desired.

STAIN BAMBOO POLE: Sand pole with heavy-gauge
sandpaper. In a well-ventilated area, using a cloth rag
or sponge brush, apply the stain to the bamboo pole
following the instructions on the can. Once the first
coat is dry, gently sand the pole again, this time with
fine-gauge sandpaper. Apply your next coat of stain,
if desired; because bamboo is a very hard wood, it can
take up to several days for each coat of stain to dry
(sanding the bamboo helps it to take the stain better
and dry more quickly). The more stain you use, the
darker the color will be.

Slide pole into the ribbon loops and hang Board
on wall.

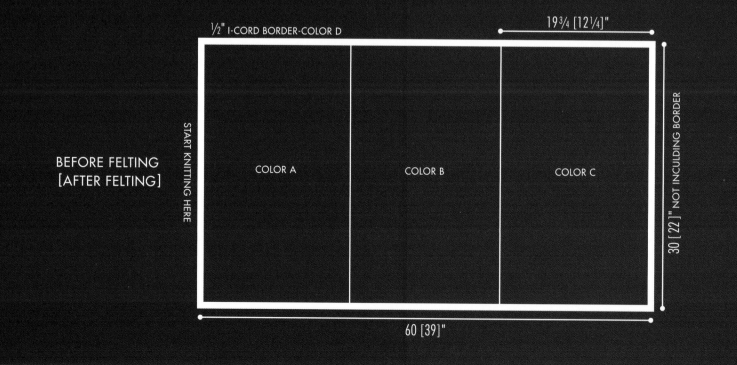

BULLETIN BOARD

½" I-CORD BORDER-COLOR D

19¾ [12¼]"

START KNITTING HERE

BEFORE FELTING
[AFTER FELTING]

COLOR A

COLOR B

COLOR C

30 [22]" NOT INCULDING BORDER

60 [39]"

A DREAM KNITTING DAY

THE DREAM
In your *AlterKnits* notebook, describe a dream knitting day, a day during
which you can indulge your passion for knitting without any boundaries or limitations.
You can fly anywhere, money is no object, and anyone you like can join you.

HERE'S MY DREAM KNITTING DAY
I wake up in a villa in Tuscany. I am there with a few of my closest knitting buddies.
We knit while enjoying breakfast out on the terrace. Midmorning we go for a leisurely bike ride,
stop and have a picnic lunch—and knit. After lunch, we time-travel ourselves to Paris
where we intermittently shop the flea markets and knit in fabulous cafés. We retire to a beautiful
penthouse apartment full of big overstuffed furniture and opulent fabrics overlooking the city.
Dinner is catered and consists of everyone's favorite things to eat and drink. We knit
and talk late into the evening, inspired by the time spent together.

THE REALITY
After writing down your fantasy, think about what you wrote and figure out if any piece
of it might be realistic. For example, I could suggest to my knitting friends
that we take a trip to Italy or France. Or, if time or money prevents us from actually traveling,
I could plan a fantasy-themed evening of knitting at my home. While we're
knitting, we could listen to Italian or French music, watch an Italian or French movie,
and eat Italian or French food.

Laptop Cases

I USE A LAPTOP ALL THE TIME —— OFTEN TRANSPORTING IT FROM PLACE TO PLACE —— AND, FOR A LONG TIME, I SEARCHED FOR A CARRYING CASE THAT FELT LIKE IT reflected my artsy aesthetic. FINALLY, I REALIZED THAT IT WOULD BE easier as well as less expensive to make one myself. I WANTED MY CASE TO HAVE VERTICAL STRIPES, BUT DIDN'T WANT TO HAVE TO MANAGE A LOT OF DIFFERENT COLORS AT THE SAME TIME, WHICH SEEMED LIKE A DILEMMA UNTIL I changed my perspective: I KNIT THE STRIPES HORIZONTALLY, WHICH MEANT I WAS ONLY DEALING WITH ONE COLOR AT A TIME, BUT THEN TURNED THE FABRIC NINETY DEGREES BEFORE SEWING THE CASE TOGETHER, THUS FINISHING WITH THE VERTICAL STRIPES I DESIRED FROM THE START.

FINISHED MEASUREMENTS

SMALL (BLUES/GREENS):
20" x 44" before felting; *13" x 14½" after felting

MEDIUM (PINK):
25" x 50½" before felting; *14" x 17½" after felting

LARGE (MULTI):
25" x 57½" before felting; *18½" x 17½" after felting

*Note: For after-felting measurements, width was measured at the base of the case; the height measurement was taken from the center bottom of case and center of handle. The curve at the top of the case can be exaggerated, if desired, by shaping it when the case is drying.

YARN

SMALL: Brown Sheep Lamb's Pride Worsted (85% wool, 15% mohair; 190 yards/4 ounces): 2 skeins each in 3 colors. Shown in #M113 oregano (A), #M52 spruce (B), #M42 twilight (C).

MEDIUM: Cascade Pastaza (50% llama, 50% wool; 132 yards/100 grams): 2 skeins each in 3 colors; 1 skein in fourth color. Shown in #50 burnt orange (A), #49 bing cherry (B), #10 russet (C), #1017 pink (D).

LARGE: Brown Sheep Lamb's Pride Worsted (85% wool/ 15% mohair; 190 yards/4 ounces): 3 skeins each in 4 colors. Shown in #M26 medieval red (A), #M185 aubergine (B), #M23 fuchsia (C), #M113 oregano (D).

NEEDLES

One set straight needles size US 10½ (6.5 mm)
Change needle size if necessary to obtain the correct gauge.

NOTIONS

Yarn needle, dressmaker's chalk, scissors, ruler

GAUGE

15 sts and 19 rows = 4" in Stockinette stitch (St st) using Cascade Pastaza
14 sts and 20 rows = 4" in Stockinette stitch (St st) using Lamb's Pride Worsted

STRIPE SEQUENCES

Note: If you want a bag exactly as shown in photo, follow the appropriate stripe sequence given. Alternatively, make up your own stripe sequence.

SMALL: In St st, work 6 rows A, 4B, 3C, 2A, 7C, 4A, 3B, 3C, 5A, 2C, 3A, 4B, 5C, 3A, 2B, 3C, 7A, 5C, 3B, 4A, 2B, 3C, 3A, 3C, 7B, 5A, 4C, 2B, 3A, 2B, 5C, 3A, 3C, 4B, 5A, 3C, 2B, 2A, 3B, 4C, 5A, 3B, 2C, 3A, 2B, 5C, 6A, 3B, 2A, 3C, 4A, 4B, 3C, 3A, 2C, 3B, 4C, 4A, 2B, 3C.

MEDIUM: In St st, work 6 rows B, 2D, 5A, 3C, 2B, 2A, 5C, 4D, 3A, 2C, 7B, 3D, 2C, 3B, 5A, 2D, 5C, 3B, 3D, 3C, 2A, 3C, 2D, 5B, 5A, 3D, 6C, 3A, 7B, 3D, 3A, 5C, 2A, 5B, 3D, 3B, 4C, 2A, 3D, 5B, 4D, 4A, 4C, 3B, 3D, 6C, 2A, 3B, 5D, 2B, 3C, 3A, 3D, 7B, 4C, 2A, 4D, 4B, 3C, 2D, 5B, 3A, 2C, 3D, 5C.

LARGE: In St st, work 4 rows A, 2D, 3B, 5A, 2C, 4D, 2B, 3A, 5C, 4B, 2D, 5A, 2D, 3B, 3C, 2A, 6B, 3D, 2C, 3B, 5D, 2C, 5A, 3B,3D, 5C, 3B, 5D, 3A, 2C, 5B, 3A, 3C, 3D, 2B, 3C, 5A, 4B, 5D, 5C, 2D, 3B, 4A, 2C, 4D, 2B, 3A, 2C, 2A, 3B, 3D, 5C, 2B, 2D, 5A, 2B, 5D, 3C, 4B, 2D, 3A, 2C, 4B, 3D, 6A, 3C, 2B, 3A, 5D, 2C, 3B, 6C, 2A, 5D, 3C, 4B, 3A, 2D, 2C, 3B, 2A, 4D, 2B, 4C, 3B.

LAPTOP CASE

Using A, CO 65 (80, 80) sts and begin St st and Stripe sequence. Work even until piece measures 44 (50½, 57½)" from the beginning. BO all sts.

FINISHING

Fold piece in half with RS's together so that it measures 18½" x 22" (21¼" x 25¼", 22¾" x 28¾"). With yarn threaded on a yarn needle, sew side and lower edge seam as shown in diagram at right. Flatten the bottom of case; sew a short seam across the triangular flap at each side, approximately 1½" from end of each triangle point, to form bottom and side gussets for case. Weave in loose ends.

FELTING

Felt the case following the instructions on page 113.

HANDLES

Lay case flat. Using dressmaker's chalk, draw a horizontal line approximately 2" down from the open (top) edge of case and 5½ (5½, 7)" in length in the center of case on both sides; cut along lines to create handles.

LAPTOP CASE

BEFORE FELTING

BO EDGE—SEW TO CO EDGE

FOLD LINE

OPEN EDGE

BOTTOM SEAM

44 (50½, 57½)"

CO EDGE—SEW TO BO EDGE

18½ (21¼, 22¾)"

1½"

SEW | BOTTOM SEAM | SEW

GUSSET

[AlterExercise]
UNBLOCK YOUR CREATIVE PATH

Do this exercise on your own or with a group.

ASK YOURSELF
What prevents you from being as creative
as you want to be? Write your
answers on index cards (one answer per card).
Put all the cards in a paper bag.

THROW AWAY THE PAPER BAG.

"THE capacity for delight IS THE GIFT OF PAYING attention."

—JULIA CAMERON

PDA Cases

THESE quick-to-knit BAGS DOUBLE AS PDA CASES AND MINI SATCHELS, perfect for outings WHEN ALL YOU WANT TO TAKE ALONG IS IDENTIFICATION, KEYS, AND SOME MONEY. THEY ARE KNITTED IN ONE COLOR, THEN FELTED AND, IF DESIRED, embellished with embroidery. TWO OPTIONS ARE GIVEN FOR THE CLOSURE (EITHER A SNAP OR A BUTTON AND BUTTON LOOP) AND FOR THE HANDLE: YOU CAN EITHER PERMANENTLY ATTACH THE HANDLE TO THE BAG ON BOTH SIDES (OPTION A), OR YOU CAN PERMANENTLY ATTACH IT ON ONE SIDE, THEN ATTACH IT TO THE OTHER SIDE WITH A BUTTON (OPTION B), MAKING IT POSSIBLE TO attach your case to something else, SUCH AS A BACKPACK OR BELT LOOP.

FINISHED MEASUREMENTS
6½" x 17" before felting;
approximately 4¾" x 5¼" (folded) after felting

YARN
Cascade Pastaza (50% llama, 50% wool; 132 yards/
100 grams): 1 skein. Shown in #50 burnt orange, #10 russet,
#49 bing cherry.

NEEDLES
One set straight needles size US 10½ (6.5mm)
Two double-pointed needles (dpn) size US 10½ (6.5mm)

NOTIONS
Embroidery needle, yarn needle, stitch holder, button
and/or snap for closure, button for handle option B
Optional: Embroidery floss in contrasting color for
embellishment and closure option B, quilting pencil
or chalk for transferring freeform flower to case

GAUGE
Gauge is not critical

PDA CASE
Using straight needles, CO 25 sts; beg St st. Work even until
piece measures 17" from the beginning—approximately
80 rows.

CLOSURE OPTION A (SNAP-SHUT): (RS) BO 8 sts, do not
break yarn; place center 9 sts onto holder; join a second ball
of yarn and BO remaining 8 sts. Place sts from holder onto a
dpn; (RS) continuing in St st, work even for 4 rows, ending
with a WS row.
Next Row: (RS) K1, ssk, knit across to last 3 sts, k2tog, k1—
7 sts remain. Work even for 5 rows, ending with a WS row.
Next Row: (RS) K1, ssk, k1, k2tog, k1—5 sts remain.
Work even for 2 rows. BO remaining sts.
(This closure is shown on burnt orange and russet cases.)

CLOSURE OPTION B (BUTTON LOOP): BO 11 sts, do not
break yarn; place center 3 sts onto holder; join a second ball
of yarn and BO rem 11 sts. Place sts from holder onto a
dpn; k3.
Begin I-cord (see Special Techniques, page 114).
Work even until I-cord measures 7" from the beginning;
BO all sts. Sew end of I-cord to BO edge of case next to
original sts, forming a large loop.
(This closure is shown on bing cherry case.)

PRE-FELTING FINISHING

Fold case in half with WS's together. With RS facing, using yarn needle, beginning at lower edge, sew side seams using mattress stitch or your choice of seaming techniques. Turn case with WS facing; lay piece flat so that seam is facing you. Sew a short seam across each corner to form gussets (see diagram at right). Weave in ends.

HANDLE OPTION A (PERMANENT): Using a dpn, attach yarn at side seam; evenly pick up 5 sts. K5; do not turn. Work I-cord for 10½". BO sts and sew to opposite side of case.

HANDLE OPTION B (BUTTON-SHUT): Work handle as above; do not sew end of I-cord to opposite side of Case. Buttonhole will be cut after felting.

FELTING

Felt the case following the instructions on page 113.

POST-FELTING FINISHING

FOR CLOSURE OPTION A (SNAP-SHUT): Sew bottom part of snap to face of bag and sew top part of snap to underside of strap. Sew button in place over the top part of snap for decoration.

FOR CLOSURE OPTION B (BUTTON LOOP): Sew button in place on front of bag. Fold I-cord loop, squeezing the 2 sides of the cord together to create an opening large enough to slip around the button. Wrap embroidery floss tightly around I-cord so that the loop stays open and the desired size. When wrap length measures approximately ½", thread floss onto yarn needle and pull to center of wrap to secure.

FOR HANDLE OPTION A (PERMANENT): Proceed to Embellishments.

FOR HANDLE OPTION B (BUTTON-SHUT): Sew button to left side of bag. Carefully cut slit at end of I-cord handle approximately ½" up from end; the slit should be just large enough to let the button slide through it and stay in place.

EMBELLISHMENTS (optional)

Using embroidery needle and floss, embellish case as desired, or as shown in photo at right.

FRENCH KNOTS (shown on bing cherry case): Using color of choice, work French knots randomly on both sides of case.

FREEFORM FLOWER (shown on russet case): For this flower, let your creativity flow. Using a pencil and piece of paper, draw freeform shapes until you have one that you like, using the photos as a guide. If you don't feel confident drawing your own flower, trace the full size diagram at right and transfer to felted fabric using quilting pencil or chalk.

Using color of choice and back stitch, stitch around the shape. Using a second color, work center (see diagram and photo at right).

Shown in photo (left to right); burnt orange, russet, bing cherry cases.

PDA CASE
AND FREEFORM FLOWER

SEW   BOTTOM   SEW

GUSSET

KEY

Back stitch-Flower outline

Loose French knot

Flower center—work
4 or 5 loose French knots
around center point

Trace diagram or draw your
own shape on paper. Transfer
to lower left Front of case as
shown. Stitch as given in Key.

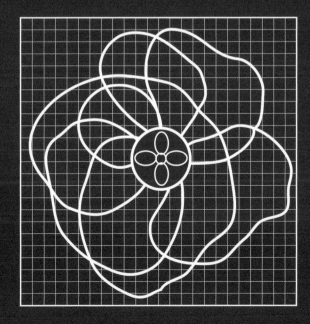

Dylan's Baby Blanket and Hat

THIS BASIC BLANKET AND HAT SET IS made unique by embellishing IT WITH FABRIC PAINT. THE STAMPED-ON POLKA-DOT PATTERN SHOWN IS super-simple. YOU MIGHT ALSO TRY STAMPING A favorite nursery rhyme ONTO THE BLANKET LINING. ONCE THE FABRIC PAINT IS HEAT-SET, BOTH PIECES ARE MACHINE-WASHABLE.

FINISHED MEASUREMENTS
Blanket: 28½" x 32¾"
Hat: 14 (16, 17¾, 19½, 21¼)" in circumference
To fit: Newborn (6–12 months, 12–18 months,
18–24 months, 24 months +)
Shown in size 6–12 months

YARN
Rowan All Seasons Cotton (60% cotton, 40% acrylic;
98 yards/50 grams): 8 skeins for Blanket; 1 skein for Hat.
Blanket shown in #192 ice blue; Hat shown in #181 plum,
#192 ice blue, #191 linen, #205 cheery.

NEEDLES
One 24" or longer circular (circ) needle size US 5 (3.5 mm)
for Blanket
One 24" or longer circ needle size US 7 (4.5 mm) for Blanket
One set of 5 double-pointed needles (dpn) size US 7 (4.5 mm)
for Hat
Change needle size if necessary to obtain the correct gauge.

NOTIONS
Stitch marker, DecoArt SoSoft fabric paint (1 fluid ounce),
Plaid (brand) Stencil "Spouncer" sponges (¾", 1¼", and
1¾"—these are 3 round sponges attached to a hand-held
dowel).
Optional: One round Styrofoam ball for painting Hat, 1 yard
100% cotton flannel for Blanket lining

GAUGE
18 sts and 25 rows = 4" in Stockinette stitch (St st) using
larger circ needle or dpn

BLANKET
Using smaller circ needle, CO 114 sts; begin Seed st.
Work even for 5 rows.
Change to larger circ needle and St st; work even until piece
measures 30¾", ending with a WS row.
Change to smaller circ needle and Seed st; work even for
4 rows.
BO all sts in pattern.

SIDE BORDERS: With RS facing, using smaller circ needle,
pick up and knit 169 sts along one side edge.
Begin Seed st; work even for 4 rows.
BO all sts in pattern. Repeat on opposite edge.

FINISHING
Weave in all ends.

PREPARE BACKING FABRIC: Wash and dry fabric to
preshrink. Cut fabric to measure 28½" x 32¾".

APPLY POLKA-DOT PATTERN: Lay fabric on hard surface
and smooth flat. Squeeze some fabric paint onto a dish or
paper plate. Dip round sponge into fabric paint and stamp
onto fabric. Continue stamping fabric, using different-sized
sponges to create desired polka-dot pattern.

Let paint dry completely. Follow instructions on fabric paint label for heat-setting your polka-dot pattern.

Once the paint has been heat-set, fold edges of fabric under ½" all the way around. Pin fabric to WS of Blanket, positioning it inside the Seed st borders; hand-stitch in place.

HAT

Using dpn, CO 64 (72, 80, 88, 96) sts; distribute sts evenly on 4 dpn. Join for working in the rnd, being careful not to twist sts; place marker (pm) for beginning of rnd.
Begin St st; work even until piece measures 4½ (5, 5½, 6, 6½)" from the beginning, or desired length, allowing for rolled edge.

SHAPE CROWN

Rnd 1: * K2, k2tog; repeat from * around—48 (54, 60, 66, 72) sts remain.
Rnd 2: * K1, k2tog; repeat from * around—32 (36, 40, 44, 48) sts remain.
Rnd 3: * K2tog; repeat from * around—16 (18, 20, 22, 24) sts remain.

Rnd 4: Repeat Rnd 3—8 (9, 10, 11, 12) sts remain.
Rnd 5: Repeat Rnd 3, end k0 (1, 0, 1, 0)—4 (5, 5, 6, 6) sts remain.
Work remaining 4 (5, 5, 6, 6) sts for 2¾"; break yarn, leaving a 4" tail. Thread tail onto yarn needle, then thread tail through remaining sts; pull snug and fasten off. Tie 2¾" length of knitting into a knot (see below). Weave in ends.

ADD POLKA DOTS TO HAT

Place your completed hat onto a round bowl or Styrofoam ball large enough to stretch the fabric smooth; if using the Styrofoam ball, place ball onto a short glass or tumbler to keep steady.

Squeeze fabric paint onto a dish or paper plate. Gently dab the round sponge into the fabric paint and press sponge onto your knitted Hat. Repeat process around the Hat, using different-sized sponges, until desired pattern is created. If you don't get the desired amount of paint coverage with one step, carefully repeat in the same place until desired coverage is achieved. Let paint dry completely.

Turn Hat inside out. Follow instructions on fabric paint label for heat-setting your polka-dot pattern.

CREATE A KNITTING
ACTION HERO

Write about or sketch yourself as a knitting action hero in your *AlterKnits* notebook.
Ask your knitting friends to do the same, then invite everyone to get together to
share the results. You're sure to laugh, you'll probably learn something new about each other,
and you may discover that you can make some of your "hero" ideas a reality.

WHAT IS YOUR NAME?
WHAT PLANET ARE YOU FROM?
WHAT ARE YOUR SUPER-HUMAN POWERS?
WHAT DOES YOUR COSTUME LOOK LIKE?
WHAT IS YOUR MOTTO?
WHAT ARE YOUR SPECIAL TALENTS?

HERE I AM AS A KNITTING ACTION HERO
My name is Paisley Patience Ruffle. I come from the planet of Raglandia Norweigbo.
I can hear the cries of knitters in trouble and immediately come to their aid.
I wear a cashmere cardigan with three-quarter-length sleeves, a tutu, tights, and high-top
Converse sneakers. I wear a long, laceweight mohair tube scarf around my neck
and a crown (see pages 19 and 29) on my head. I usually carry a pair of ebony
knitting needles that double as magic wands. My motto is "DON'T FORGET TO BREATHE."
With the touch of my wand, all knitting mistakes are corrected.

"Art evokes the
   mystery WITHOUT
WHICH THE WORLD WOULD
      NOT EXIST."

— RENÉ MAGRITTE

Cardigans for Clark and Lily

· — · —

BASIC EMBROIDERY STITCHES jazz up this colorful caridgan FOR BOYS AND GIRLS. WHEN DESIGNING IT, I WAS CAREFUL TO KEEP THE COLORS AND THE MOTIFS GENDER-NEUTRAL SO THAT IT COULD BE EASILY handed down from sibling to sibling (OR OTHER FAMILY MEMBER) WITHOUT WORRYING ABOUT IT BEING TOO MASCULINE OR FEMININE. Unlike traditional cardigans, THE BOTTOM OF THIS ONE IS KNIT IN THREE SEPARATE PANELS (TWO FRONTS AND A BACK). THE EMBROIDERY IS WORKED AT THE END AND IS, OF COURSE, OPTIONAL.

FINISHED MEASUREMENTS
24 (26, 28, 30, 32)" chest, buttoned
To fit Child's size 2 (4, 6, 8, 10)
Shown in size 26" (see left) and size 30" (see page 75)

YARN
Louet Gems Topaz (100% wool; 175 yards/100 grams):
2 (2, 3, 4, 4) skeins main color (A), 1 skein each of three contrasting colors. Shown in size 26"(see left) in Colorway 1
—#2014 champagne (A), #2554 willow (B), #2524 grape (C), #2474 terra cotta (D); in size 30"(see page 75) in Colorway 2—#2534 caribou (A), #2474 terra cotta (B), #2364 linen grey (C), #2484 aqua (D).

NEEDLES
One 29" circular (circ) needle size US 8 (5.5 mm)
Change needle size if necessary to obtain the correct gauge.

NOTIONS
Stitch holders, stitch markers, yarn needle, six 3/8" buttons

GAUGE
18 sts and 21 rows = 4" in Stockinette stitch (St st)

NOTE
To create smooth edges on garment pieces, work edge (selvage) stitches throughout patterns, as follows:
Slip the first st knitwise on every row, and purl the last st.

LOWER EDGE PANELS
BACK: Using A CO 53 (57, 61, 65, 69) sts; begin St st.
(RS) Work 5 rows St st, ending with a RS row.
(WS) Change to B; purl 1 row.
(RS) Change to Seed st; work 2 rows.
(RS) Change to St st; work 2 rows.
Continue as follows:
Row 1 (RS): Slip 1 (edge st), k4 (2, 4, 2, 4)–B, * k1–C, p1–B, k1–C, k5–B; repeat from * across, end last repeat k4 (2, 4, 2, 4)–B, p1–B (edge st).
Row 2: Slip 1 (edge st), p4 (2, 4, 2, 4)–B, * p1–C, p1–B, p1–C, p5–B; repeat from * across, end last repeat p5 (3, 5, 3, 5)–B.
Rows 3–5: Repeat Rows 1 and 2 once, then work Row 1 once more.
Rows 6 and 7: Using B, work in St st.
Place sts on holder.

RIGHT FRONT: Using A, CO 27 (29, 31, 33, 35) sts.
Work as for Back for 10 rows, ending with a WS row.
Continue as follows:
Row 1 (RS): Slip 1 (edge st), k2 (4, 1, 3, 2)–B, * k1–C,
p1–B, k1–C, k5–B; repeat from * across, end last repeat
k4 (4, 1, 1, 4)–B, p1–B (edge st)
Row 2: Slip 1 (edge st), p4 (4, 1, 1, 4)–B, * p1–C, p1–B, p1–C, p5–B;
repeat from * across, end last repeat p3 (5, 2, 4, 3)–B.
Rows 3–7: Work as for Back.

LEFT FRONT: Work as for Back for 10 Rows, ending with a WS row.
Continue as follows:
Row 1 (RS): Slip 1 (edge st), k4 (4, 1, 1, 4)–B, * k1–C, p1–B, k1 – C,
k5–B, repeat from * across, end last repeat k2 (4, 1, 3, 2)–B, p1–B
(edge st).
Row 2: Slip 1 (edge st), p2 (4, 1, 3, 2)–B, * p1–C, p1–B, p1–C, p5–B;
repeat from * across, end last repeat p5 (5, 2, 2, 5)–B.
Rows 3–7: Work as for Back.

BODY
Using D, CO 107 (115, 123, 131, 139) sts; work edge sts throughout.
Begin Seed st; work even for 2 rows, ending with a WS row.
Change to St st.

JOINING ROW: (RS) Place sts for lower panels on a spare needle,
ready to work a RS row (begin right Front, then Back, then left
Front). With RS of panels facing WS of Body, * knit 1 st from Body
together with 1 st from lower panel; repeat from * across, joining
lower panels to Body.
Continuing in St st for remainder of piece, work even until piece
measures 3¼" from the beginning of Body.
Change to A; work even until piece measures 6 (6¾, 7½, 7¾, 8)"
from beginning of Body, ending with a WS row.

DIVIDING ROW: (RS) Work 27 (29, 31, 33, 35) sts for right Front,
place sts on holder; work 53 (57, 61, 65, 69) sts for Back;
place remaining 27 (29, 31, 33, 35) sts for left Front on holder.

BACK: Continuing on Back sts only, work even until piece
measures 11 (12, 13, 13½, 14)" from beginning of Body. BO all sts;
pm each side of center 27 (29, 31, 33, 35) sts for neck.

LEFT FRONT: Return 27 (29, 31, 33, 35) sts for left Front to needle,
ready to work a RS row. Join yarn at armhole edge; work across.

SHAPE NECK: (WS) At neck edge, decrease 1 st every row 4 (4, 6, 6, 8)
times, every other row 10 (11, 10, 11, 10) times—13 (14, 15, 16, 17)
sts remain for shoulder.
Work even until piece measures same as Back to shoulders.
BO all sts.

RIGHT FRONT: Return 27 (29, 31, 33, 35) sts for right Front
to needle, ready to work a WS row. Join yarn at armhole edge;
work across. Work as for left Front, reversing shaping.

SLEEVES
LEFT SLEEVE: Using B, CO 24 (26, 28, 30, 32) sts; begin Seed st;
work even for 2 rows, ending with a WS row. Change to St st; work
even until piece measures 1½" from the beginning, ending with a
WS row.

SHAPE SLEEVE: (RS) Increase 1 st each side this row, then every
other row 7 (2 , 0, 0, 0) times, every 4 rows 3 (8, 6, 5, 2) times,
every 6 rows 0 (0, 4, 5, 8) times— 46 (48, 50, 52, 54) sts; and AT THE
SAME TIME, when piece measures 4 (4½, 5, 5½, 6)" from the
beginning, change to A for remainder of Sleeve. When shaping is
completed, work even until piece measures 7½ (9½, 11½, 12½, 13¼)"
from beginning. BO all sts.

RIGHT SLEEVE: Using C, CO and work as for left Sleeve until
piece measures 3¾ (4¼, 4¾, 5¼, 5¾)" from the beginning.
For Colorway 1, add 2-row stripe, as follows:
Change to B; work 1 row.
Change to D; work 1 row.
Change to A for remainder of Sleeve; work as for left Sleeve.

FINISHING
Block all pieces. With yarn threaded on yarn needle, sew
shoulder seams. Sew Sleeves into armholes; sew Sleeve seams.
Weave in loose ends.

BUTTON BAND: With RS facing, beginning at lower right Front,
pick up and knit 132 (144, 154, 162, 188) sts evenly along Front and
neck edges. Knit 1 row.
Begin Seed st; work 1 row.

BUTTONHOLES: Pm for 6 buttonholes on right or left Front edge. Place first marker ½" from lower edge, last marker ½" from beginning of neck shaping, remaining 4 evenly spaced between. Continuing in Seed st, work buttonholes as follows: work to first marker, *[ssk, yo] for buttonhole, work to next marker; repeat from * 4 times, work remaining buttonhole, work to end. Sew buttons opposite buttonholes.

EMBROIDERY (see photos and diagram): Using C threaded onto yarn needle, work ½" Satin st motifs evenly spaced across color change on Fronts, Back, and left Sleeve for Colorway 1 (right Sleeve is shown with 2-row Stripe); work across Fronts, Back, and both Sleeves for Colorway 2. Using B, work 1 duplicate stitch (see Special Techniques, page 113) 2 sts above upper end of Satin st motifs.

As shown in the photographs, work daisy chain st at center Back and work one double-wrap French knot at center of daisy OR work Spiral motif in running stitch and satin stitch at center Back.

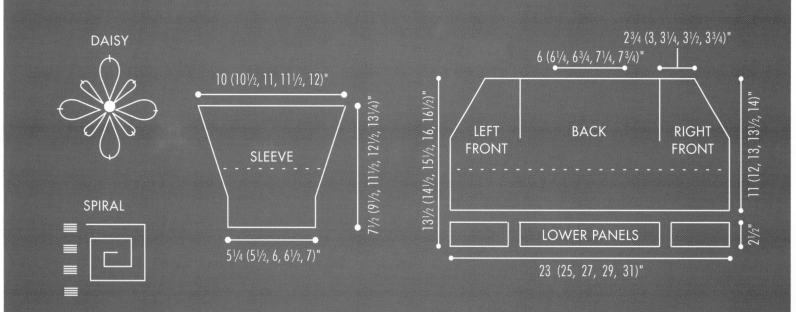

CARDIGANS FOR CLARK AND LILY

DAISY

SPIRAL

SLEEVE

10 (10½, 11, 11½, 12)"

7½ (9½, 11½, 12½, 13¾)"

5¼ (5½, 6, 6½, 7)"

2¾ (3, 3¼, 3½, 3¾)"

6 (6¼, 6¾, 7¼, 7¾)"

LEFT FRONT   BACK   RIGHT FRONT

13½ (14½, 15½, 16, 16½)"

11 (12, 13, 13½, 14)"

LOWER PANELS

2½"

23 (25, 27, 29, 31)"

ROUND ROBIN

This exercise works best with at least three people. It is meant to encourage
exploration of new and different combinations of yarn and needles.

TO GET READY
Put a collection of different-sized knitting needles in a paper bag (at least
two needles for each participant; for example, if three people are doing the exercise,
put at least six needles in the bag).

Put a collection of different types of yarn in a second paper bag
(at least one ball of yarn for each participant; for example, if three people are doing
the exercise, put at least three yarns in the bag). Be sure to include
yarns of different fibers, weights, and textures.

TO START
Ask each knitter to close his or her eyes and pick two needles (they don't need to be the
same size) and one yarn from the bags, and then (with eyes opened) start knitting
a swatch in any stitch pattern desired. After 10 to 15 minutes, have each knitter give the
needle in his/her right hand to the person on his/her right. After about
10 to 15 more minutes, have each knitter hand the needle in his/her left hand to the
person on his or her right. Continue going around until everyone has
experimented with a variety of needle sizes.

"LIFE SHRINKS OR EXPANDS
in proportion to
one's courage."

—ANAIS NIN

Paper Lanterns

Two fabulous papery Japanese yarns (ONE PURE LINEN, THE OTHER A BLEND OF LINEN AND NYLON) INSPIRED THESE translucent, quick-to-knit lanterns, WHICH I'VE USED TO COVER ORDINARY CHRISTMAS LIGHTS. THEY create a festive atmosphere WHEREVER YOU PLACE THEM.

FINISHED MEASUREMENTS
Using 1 strand of Shosenshi Paper: 1½" square
Using 1 strand each Shosenshi Paper and Paper Moire:
1¾" wide x 1½" tall

YARN
Habu Textiles Shosenshi Paper (100% linen; 280 yards /
3 ounces): 1 skein. Shown in #115 gray / beige.

Habu Textiles Paper Moire (50% linen, 50% nylon; 311 yards/
½ ounce): 1 ball. Shown in #05 mocha.

Note: This amount of yarn will make 40 – 50 lanterns.

NEEDLES
One set of 5 double-pointed needles (dpn) size US 8 (5mm)
Change needle size if necessary to obtain the correct gauge.

MATERIALS
8-foot strand or desired length decorative indoor
Christmas lights

NOTIONS
Yarn needle, stitch markers

GAUGE
21 sts and 24 rows = 4" in Stockinette stitch (St st) using
Shosenshi Paper
18 sts and 24 rows = 4" in St st using Shosenshi Paper and
Paper Moire together

NOTE
Using dpn helps to define the "edges" of each square lantern; pinching the sides of the lantern, where you have moved from one dpn to the next, further defines the edges.

SHOSENSHI PAPER LANTERNS
Using 1 strand Shosenshi Paper, CO 32 sts, dividing evenly on each of 4 needles—8 sts each needle. Join for working in the round, being careful not to twist sts; place marker (pm) for beginning of rnd. Begin St st; work even until piece measures 1½" from the beginning. Purl 1 rnd.

SHAPE TOP: Rnd 1: * Slip 1, k1, psso, k4, k2tog; repeat from * 3 times—24 sts remain.
Rnd 2: Knit.
Rnd 3: * Slip 1, k1, psso, k2, k2tog; repeat from * 3 times—16 sts remain.
Rnd 4: Knit.
Rnd 5: * Slip 1, k1, psso, k2tog; repeat from * 3 times—8 sts remain.

Cut yarn, leaving an 8" tail. With tail threaded onto yarn needle, gather live sts and pull tight, leaving a small opening for bulb. Weave in loose ends. Slip the lantern over a bulb on a strand of Christmas lights.

SHOSENSHI AND PAPER MOIRE LANTERNS
Work as above, using 1 strand of Shosenshi Paper and 1 strand of Paper Moire held together.

Mixed Media Pillows

— • —

I STARTED DESIGNING THESE PILLOWS BY KNITTING ONLY WITH STRIPS OF SILK FABRIC. I LIKED THE EFFECT BUT FELT THEY NEEDED TO BE SOFTER, BOTH TO THE TOUCH AND TO THE EYE. AFTER experimenting with many different types of yarn, I DECIDED TO COMBINE THE SILK FABRIC WITH A STRAND OF MOHAIR-BLEND YARN AND A STRAND OF LINEN YARN TO create a luxurious new fabric with a more complex texture. I LET THE ENDS OF THE SILK FABRIC STICK OUT RATHER THAN WEAVING THEM IN BECAUSE I like the way they look, BUT YOU CAN WEAVE YOURS IN IF YOU PREFER A MORE PRISTINE FINISH.

FINISHED MEASUREMENTS
Small (medium, large)
16" x 12" (16" x 16", 18" x 18")

YARN AND FABRIC
Louet British Mohair (78% mohair, 13% wool, 9% nylon; 105 yards / 50 grams): 2 (3, 3) skeins. Shown in #8776 deep rich red (#1108 dark gray, #9544 olive din).

Louet Euroflax Linen Sport Weight (100% linen; 270 yards / 100 grams): 1 (2, 2) skeins. Shown in # 21036 madeira (#21026-2 moss lake, #21006 seaway mix).

44"/45" dupioni or chiffon silk fabric (100% silk): 2½ (3½, 4½) yards.
Note: Dupioni silk creates a stiffer fabric than silk chiffon.

For information on how yarn colors and fabrics are combined in pillows shown, see photo caption on page 82.

NEEDLES
One 32" long circular (circ) needle size US 17 (12 mm)
Change needle size if necessary to obtain the correct gauge.

NOTIONS
Stitch markers, cable needle (cn; size Large only), three ⅞" buttons (sizes Medium and Large only), acrylic quilting ruler, rotary cutter and mat; pillow form to fit size you are making.
Note: You may wish to cover pillow form with fabric, as pillow form may show through the knitted fabric.

GAUGE
9 sts and 12 rows = 4" in Stockinette stitch (St st)

PREPARE FABRIC
Fold fabric in half lengthwise (end to end, so that if you're starting with 2 yards fabric, folding it leaves a 1-yard length). Keep folding in half as above until entire yardage has been folded down to a 10–12" length. You'll have a piece that measures approximately 10–12" by the width of the fabric (see diagram on page 83).

CUT STRIPS
Place folded fabric on mat. *Place ruler ½" away from the end of the folded fabric as shown in diagram on page 83. Using rotary cutter and a new blade, cut through all layers of fabric; you now have a ½" strip of fabric that measures the length of the beginning yardage—for this example, 2 yards.

Repeat from * until all your fabric has been cut into ½" strips. Knot ends of strips together, and wind into a ball.

NOTE
All pillows are worked using 3 strands held together—1 strand of mohair, 1 strand of linen, and 1 strand of fabric, unless otherwise noted.

PILLOW BODY
SMALL AND MEDIUM: Using one strand each of mohair, linen, and fabric held together, CO 74 (74) sts. Join for working in the rnd, being careful not to twist sts; place marker (pm) for beginning of rnd. Begin St st; work even until piece measures 12¼ (16)" from the beginning.

LARGE: Working as for Small, CO 82 sts. Join for working in the rnd, being careful not to twist sts; place marker (pm) for beginning of rnd.
Begin Stitch pattern as follows:
Rnds 1–3: Knit, pm after St 41 on first row (beginning of rnd marker is after St 82).
Rnd 4: < K7, * [knit next 3 sts, slip sts to cn, (wrap yarn clockwise around these 3 sts) 3 times, return sts to right-hand needle], k5; repeat from * twice across next 16 sts, repeat [to] once more across next 3 sts, k7 >; slip marker (sm); repeat < to > once for second half of pillow.
Rnds 5–7: Knit.
Rnd 8: < K3, * [knit next 3 sts, slip sts to cn, (wrap yarn clockwise around these 3 sts) 3 times, return sts to right-hand needle], k5; repeat from * 3 times across next 24 sts, repeat [to] once more across next 3 sts, k3; sm; repeat < to > once for second half of pillow.
Repeat Rnds 1–8 for Stitch pattern.
Work even until piece measures 18" from the beginning.

FINISHING
SMALL: BO all sts. Turn piece inside out, so that Rev St st side becomes the RS. Weave in yarn/fabric ends or pull to RS. Seam one open end together; insert pillow form; seam remaining end together.

MEDIUM: Button band: Using 2 strands linen and 1 strand fabric, begin Seed st; work even for 2 rnds.

Buttonholes: Continuing in Seed st, work 8 sts, * [yo, k2tog] for Buttonhole, work 9 sts; repeat from * twice, work to end of rnd. Work even for 1 rnd; BO all sts in pattern.

Weave in yarn/fabric ends or pull to RS. Sew bottom seam; sew buttons opposite buttonholes. Insert pillow form; button top edge.

LARGE: Button band: Using 2 strands mohair and 2 strands linen, work 2 rnds Seed st, dec 2 sts evenly on first rnd—80 sts remain.

Buttonholes: Continuing in Seed st, work 9 sts, * [yo, k2tog] for Buttonhole, work 8 sts; repeat from * twice, work to marker; sm; work in Seed st as established to end of rnd. Work even for 1 rnd; BO all sts loosely in pattern.

Weave in yarn/fabric ends or pull to RS. Sew bottom seam; sew buttons opposite buttonholes. Insert pillow form; button top edge.

Shown in photo far right (top to bottom): size small in deep rich red mohair, madeira linen, and dupioni silk fabric; size medium in dark gray mohair, moss lake linen, and silk chiffon fabric; size large in olive din mohair, seaway mix linen, and dupioni silk fabric.

MIXED MEDIA PILLOW

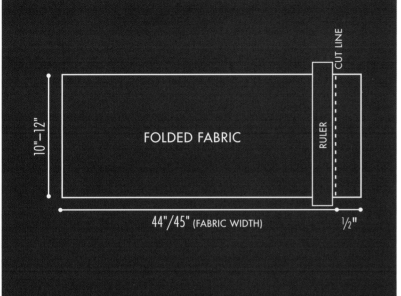

CUT LINE

RULER

FOLDED FABRIC

10"–12"

44"/45" (FABRIC WIDTH)

½"

[AlterExercise]

KNITTING ON A DESERT ISLAND

In your *AlterKnits* notebook,
write down what you would take to knit and
why if you were going to live on a
deserted island by yourself or with just a few
people for one month. Ask your knitting
friends the same question.

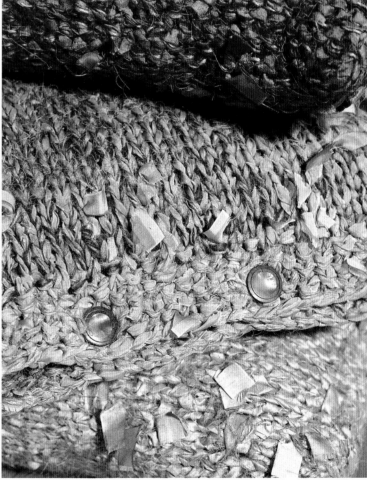

"I haven't failed, I've found 10,000 ways that don't work."

— BENJAMIN FRANKLIN

Bridgetown T-Shirt Rugs

— • —

THESE SIMPLE RUGS KNIT UP QUICKLY IN GARTER STITCH ON SIZE 19 NEEDLES AND GIVE YOU SOMETHING creative and useful TO DO WITH T-SHIRTS THAT HAVE PASSED THEIR PRIME. IF YOU DON'T HAVE ENOUGH T-SHIRTS ON HAND OR IF YOU NEED DIFFERENT COLORS, ASK YOUR FRIENDS AND FAMILY FOR DONATIONS OR check for some at your local thrift stores.

THE COLORS I CHOSE FOR THESE TWO RUGS WERE inspired by the view from my studio window, WHICH LOOKS OUT ACROSS THE WILLAMETTE RIVER TO THE SKYLINE OF DOWNTOWN PORTLAND. THE MULTICOLORED VERSION (SEE PAGE 112) REPRESENTS THE ENTIRE SKYLINE. FOR THE VERSION AT LEFT, I ISOLATED JUST THE REDS AND PINKS.

FINISHED MEASUREMENTS

Small (see page 112): 24" x 37"
Large (see left): 33" x 51"

MATERIALS

Approx 18 (26) adult Large or X-Large T-Shirts, cut into ½" strips
Note: A men's large T-shirt, cut into ½" strips, yields approximately 23 yards "yarn."

NEEDLES

One 40" circular (circ) needle size US 19 (15 mm)
Change needle size if necessary to obtain correct gauge.

NOTIONS

Sewing thread, sewing needle, 3½ (5) yards ⅞"-wide bias tape (optional)

GAUGE

Approximately 7 sts and 13 rows = 4" in Garter stitch

PREPARE T-SHIRTS

Beginning at the hem of a T-shirt, begin cutting ½" strips as follows:
At side seam, cut ½" into T-shirt hem. Turn scissors 90 degrees and continue cutting just above the hem. As you work around to side seam, where you began, continue cutting around the body of the T-shirt in a circular fashion on a slight diagonal. Cut the body of the shirt into one long strip, from the hem to just under the arms; discard the sleeves and top part of the T-shirt. Wind the strip of fabric into a ball. Repeat until all of your T-shirts have been transformed into "yarn."

CHANGING BALLS OF YARN: As you come to the end of a ball, leave a 3" tail; begin a new ball, also leaving a 3" tail, and continue in pattern as established.

RUG

CO 46 (60) sts; begin Garter st. Work even until piece measures 37" (51") from the beginning. BO all sts.

FINISHING

Knot tails where you joined a new ball of yarn; weave in ends. Sew bias tape around edge of Rug, if desired.

"THERE IS ONLY ONE valuable
THING IN ART; THE THING YOU
cannot explain."
—GEORGE BRAQUE

Abstract Cardigan

I'VE LONG ADMIRED THE WORK OF ABSTRACT ARTISTS LIKE Wassily Kandinksy, Paul Klee, Joan Miro, AND Lee Kranser. IN THE PAST I HAVE WORKED SHAPES FROM THEIR ARTWORKS INTO PROJECTS (A RATHER LITERAL INTERPRETATION), BUT FOR THIS CARDIGAN, I DECIDED TO LEARN FROM THEM BY ACTUALLY knitting more abstractly. BREAKING WITH TRADITION, I KNITTED EACH OF THE THREE MAIN PARTS OF THE CARDIGAN (FRONTS, BACK, AND SLEEVES) IN A DIFFERENT YARN AT A DIFFERENT GAUGE. THIS MAKES THE RESULT UNIQUE AND ALSO MAKES THE PROCESS OF KNITTING ESPECIALLY INTERESTING. No more boredom with the same yarn throughout.

FINISHED MEASUREMENTS
34 (38, 42)" chest
Shown in size 38"

YARN AND RIBBON
BACK: Rowan Summer Tweed (70% silk, 30% cotton; 118 yards / 50 grams): 3 (3, 4) skeins main color (A), 1 (1, 1) skein contrast color (B). Shown in #520 hurricane (A), #534 delicious (B).

FRONTS: Rowan Wool Cotton (50% Merino wool, 50% cotton; 123 yards / 50 grams): 3 (3, 4) balls main color (C), 1 ball each in 3 contrast colors. Shown in #910 gypsy (C), #957 lavish (D), #903 misty (E), #941 clear (F).
Note: Kid Silk Haze (G) is also used on Front; sleeve yardage is sufficient for both sleeves and right Front.

SLEEVES: Rowan Kid Silk Haze (70% super kid mohair, 30% silk; 229 yards / 25 grams): 2 (2, 3) balls. Shown in #605 smoke (G). Use 2 strands held together for Sleeves; 1 strand for right Front.

RIBBON: 6¾ yards ⅜"-wide silk ribbon (18 pieces cut to 5½"; 18 pieces cut to 8"), plus (optional) ¾ yard additional ribbon for body.

NEEDLES
One set straight needles size US 5 (3.75 mm)
One set straight needles size US 6 (4 mm)
One set straight needles size US 7 (4.5 mm)
One set straight needles size US 8 (5 mm)
One set straight needles size US 10½ (6.5 mm)
Change needle size if necessary to obtain the correct gauge.

NOTIONS
Yarn needle, stitch holders, stitch markers

GAUGES
BACK: 17 sts and 22 rows = 4" in Stockinette stitch (St st)
FRONT: 23 sts and 28 rows = 4" in St st
SLEEVES: 15 sts and 20 rows = 4" in St st using 2 strands of G held together

To create smooth edges on garment pieces, work edge (selvage) stitches throughout pattern, as follows: Slip the first st knitwise on every row, and knit the last st.

When working facings, cast on with larger needles, then change to smaller needles to make it easier to knit the CO edge together for the hem.

BACK

FACING: Using size 8 needles and B, CO 72 (82, 90) sts. Change to size 7 needles and begin St st. (WS) Work even for 2 rows, ending with a RS row. (WS) Knit 1 row.

HEM: Change to size 8 needles; knit 2 rows, ending with a WS row (fold line).
(RS) Change to St st; work even for 2 rows.

JOIN FACING TO HEM: (RS) Fold facing to WS of piece, with CO edge parallel to needle; in St st, knit first st on left-hand needle together with first CO st of facing, * knit next st on needle together with next CO st; repeat from * across, joining facing to hem. Continuing in St st, work even until piece measures 2½" from fold line. Change to 1 strand G and 1 strand E; work 2 rows even.

NEXT ROW: Work 29 sts as established; change to A and work to end. Continuing with A in St st, work even until piece measures 11¼ (11¾, 12¼)" from fold line, ending with a WS row.

SHAPE ARMHOLES: (RS) BO 4 (5, 6) sts at beginning of next 2 rows —64 (72, 78) sts remain.
(RS) Dec 1 st each side this row, then every 4 rows 3 (4, 5) times— 56 (62, 66) sts remain.
Work even until armhole measures 6½ (7, 7½)" from beginning of shaping, ending with a WS row; pm each side of center 32 sts.

SHAPE NECK: (RS) Work across to marker; join a second ball of A and BO center 32 sts, work to end—12 (15, 17) sts rem each side for shoulders. Working both sides at same time, work even until armhole measures 7¾ (8¼, 8¾)" from beginning of shaping. BO all sts.

LEFT FRONT

PANEL A: Using size 7 needles and D, CO 56 (60, 64) sts.
Row 1 (RS): K3, * p2, k2; repeat from * across, end last repeat k3.
Row 2: P3, * k2, p2; repeat from * across, end last repeat p3.
Repeat Rows 1 and 2 until piece measures 4" from the beginning, ending with a WS row.
Next Row (RS): K1, * k2tog, p2tog; repeat from * to last 3 sts, end k2tog, k1—29 (31, 33) sts remain. Place sts onto holder.

PANEL B: Using size 6 needles and E, CO 24 (28, 32) sts; begin St st. Work even until piece measures 2¼" from the beginning, ending with a RS row; place sts on holder.

UPPER FRONT: Using size 6 needles and C, CO 46 (52, 58) sts; begin Seed st. Work even for 5 rows, ending with a WS row. Change to St st.

JOINING ROWS: (RS): Place Panel A sts from holder onto a spare needle, ready to work a RS row; with RS of Panel A facing WS of Upper Front, needles parallel and pointing in the same direction, * knit 1 st from upper Front together with 1 st from Panel A; repeat from * 28 (30, 32) times (all sts of Panel A worked together with upper Front sts), work to end.

NEXT ROW: (WS) Place Panel B sts from holder onto a spare needle, ready to work a WS row; with RS of Panel B facing WS of Upper Front, needles parallel and pointing in the same direction, * purl 1 st from upper Front together with 1 st from Panel B; repeat from * 23 (27, 31) times (all sts of Panel B worked together with upper Front sts; 7 sts of Panel B overlap Panel A), work to end.

Continuing in St st, work even until upper Front measures 6½ (7, 7½)" from the beginning, ending with a WS row.

SHAPE ARMHOLE: As for Back at beginning of RS rows— 38 (42, 46) sts remain. Work even until armhole measures 3 (3½, 3¾)" from beginning of armhole shaping, ending with a RS row.

SHAPE NECK: (WS) At neck edge, decrease 1 st every row 26 (27, 29) times—12 (15, 17) sts remain for shoulder. Work even until armhole measures same as Back to shoulder. BO remaining sts.

RIGHT FRONT

PANEL A: Using size 6 needles and one strand of G, CO 46 (52, 58) sts; begin St st.
Work even until piece measures 3" from the beginning, ending with a WS row; place sts on holder.

PANEL B: Using size 6 needles and one strand of G, CO 25 (27, 29) sts; begin St st.
Work even until piece measures 2½" from the beginning, ending with a WS row; place sts on holder.

UPPER FRONT

FACING: Using size 6 needles and F, CO 46 (52, 58) sts.
Change to size 5 needles and begin St st; work even for 5 rows, ending on a RS.

HEM: (WS) Change to size 6 needles; knit 2 rows, ending with a WS row (fold line).
Next Row: Change to E and St st; work 2 rows even.
Change to C; work 1 row.

JOIN FACING TO HEM: (RS) Fold facing to WS of piece, with CO edge parallel to needle; in St st, knit first st on left-hand needle together with first CO st of facing, * knit next st on needle together with next CO st; repeat from * across, joining facing to hem. Continuing with C, work 1 row even.

JOIN PANEL A: (RS) Place Panel A sts from holder onto a spare needle, ready to work a RS row; with RS of Panel A facing WS of Upper Front, needles parallel and pointing in the same direction, * knit 1 st from upper Front together with 1 st from Panel A; repeat from * across (all sts of Panel A worked together with upper Front sts). Continuing in St st using C, work even until piece measures 5¼" from facing fold, ending with a RS row.

JOIN PANEL B: (WS) Place Panel B sts from holder onto a spare needle, ready to work a WS row; with WS of Panel B facing RS of Upper Front, needles parallel and pointing in the same direction, * purl 1 st from upper Front together with 1 st from Panel B; repeat from * 24 (26, 28) times, (all sts of Panel B worked together with upper Front sts), work to end. Continuing in St st, work even until piece measures 7¼ (7¾, 8¼)" from fold line, ending with a RS row.

SHAPE ARMHOLE AND NECK: Work as for Left Front reversing shaping.

SLEEVES
Using size 10½ needles and 2 strands G, CO 49 sts; begin St st.

SHAPE LOWER SLEEVE: (RS) Decrease 1 st each side every 4 rows 5 times; and AT THE SAME TIME, when piece measures 1" from the beginning, end with a RS row.

Continue as follows:
* SHORT ROWS (see Special Techniques, page 115):
(WS) Work across to 15 sts before end of row, wrap next st and turn (wrp-t) as follows: yb, slip 1, yf, return slipped st to left-hand needle, turn. (RS) Work across to 15 sts before end of row, wrp-t as follows: yf, slip 1, yb, return slipped st to left-hand needle, turn.

Working wraps together with wrapped sts as you come to them, continue as follows:
(WS and RS rows): Work to 12 sts before end of row, wrp-t. Work to 9 sts before end of row, wrp-t. Work to within 7 sts, wrp-t; work to within 5 sts, wrp-t; then work to within 3 sts, wrp-turn. Begin working all sts, continuing Sleeve shaping—39 sts remain.

When work measures 4" from the beginning (measured along side edge, not in Short Row area), end with a WS row.

SHAPE SLEEVE: Increase 1 st each side this row, then every 4 rows 5 (7, 9) times—51 (55, 59) sts. Work even until piece measures 12½" from beginning, ending with a WS row.

SHAPE CAP: BO 5 sts beg of next 2 rows—41 (45, 49) sts remain. Decrease 2 sts at the beginning of next 4 rows—33 (37, 41) sts remain. Decrease 1 st each side every other row 11 times—

11 (15, 19) sts remain. When piece measures 6¾" from beginning of shaping, BO all sts.

FINISHING
Sew shoulder seams. Set in Sleeves; sew Sleeve seams. Sew side seams, working from underarm to lower edge, ending seam at edge of upper Front and Back (panels are left open—both sides are intended to be uneven).

NECK: With RS facing, using size 6 needles, work as follows: Beginning at right Front, using C, pick up and knit 44 sts; using D, pick up and knit 5 sts; using E, pick up and knit 44 sts—93 sts; begin St st. Continuing as established, work 3 rows even.
Row 4: Work across 49 sts (through 5 D-sts at center Back); change to F, work to end.
Row 5: (WS) Knit 1 row (fold line), working 39 sts F, 5 sts D, and 49 sts C.

FACING: (RS) Change to size 5 needles and St st; work 1 row in established colors.
Row 2 (WS): Work 39 sts F, work 54 sts D. Work 2 more rows in established colors. BO all sts.

Fold facing to WS; beginning at left Front, sew facing in place to within 4" of right Front (this causes the facing on the right-hand side to roll forward, and was done on purpose).

BACK EMBROIDERY: Using B threaded onto yarn needle, work 3 rows of running st as shown in bottom photo on page 89.

RIBBON PLACEMENT: Thread a 5½" piece of ribbon onto yarn needle. Beginning approximately 1½" from lower edge of right or left sleeve, leaving a 1½" tail at the beginning, weave ribbon through every other row for about 1½", turn; weave end back down through ribbon in a zigzag fashion; allow any extra ribbon to hang as a tail. Repeat with 8" pieces of ribbon, beginning 3 rows over from first ribbon and 2¼" up from lower edge of sleeve to create a staggered effect. Repeat around sleeve. Work second sleeve same as first. If desired, use the same technique to apply a row of 4 ribbons of varying length to one of the cardigan Fronts.

ABSTRACT CARDIGAN

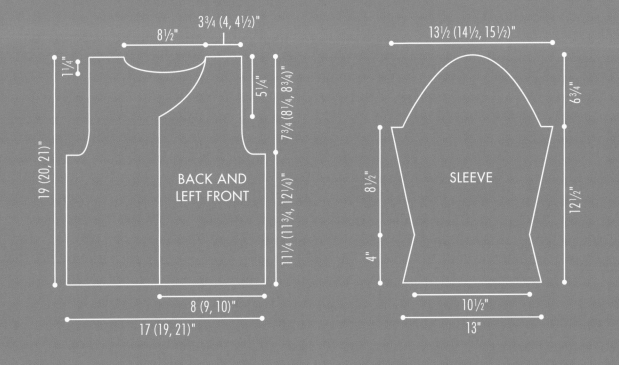

BACK AND
LEFT FRONT

8½"

3¾ (4, 4½)"

1¼"

5¼"

7¾ (8¼, 8¾)"

19 (20, 21)"

11¼ (11¾, 12¼)"

8 (9, 10)"

17 (19, 21)"

SLEEVE

13½ (14½, 15½)"

6¾"

8½"

12½"

4"

10½"

13"

[AlterExercise]
COLOR CLASS

This exercise can be done on your own, but is often more fun in a group. It is meant to encourage
experimentation with colors of yarn we might not ordinarily put together.

TO GET READY
Gather together lots of balls of different colors of scrap yarn in a similar weight and place
them in a paper bag (at least three colors of yarn for each participant; for example, if three people are doing
the exercise, put at least nine colors of yarn in the bag).

TO START
Ask each knitter to close his or her eyes and pick at least three colors of yarn from the bag, then—
with whatever needles desired (and eyes opened)—knit a swatch incorporating all of the yarns chosen.
When everyone has finished, discuss the results.

"YOU DON'T UNDERSTAND ANYTHING
UNTIL YOU learn it more than
one way."

—MARVIN MINSKY

Unisex Deconstructed Pullover

MY GOAL WITH THIS SWEATER (SHOWN ON THE MAN IN THE PHOTO) WAS TO design a unique garment constructed nontraditionally. I USED DIFFERENT COLORS TO CREATE the illusion of a layered garment; I VARIED THE SEQUENCE OF COLORS FROM ONE SLEEVE TO THE OTHER; I USED STOCKINETTE AND REVERSE STOCKINETTE STITCHES asymmetrically ON THE BACK; AND I SEWED THE SWEATER TOGETHER SO THE SEAMS WERE EXPOSED.

FINISHED MEASUREMENTS
40 (44, 48)" chest
Shown in size 48"

YARN
GGH Via Mala (100% merino wool; 77 yards/50 grams):
15 (16, 17) balls main color (A), 3 (4, 4) balls for Front panel
(B), 1 (1, 1) contrast color (C). Shown in #25 slate blue (A),
#1 brown (B), #13 navy (C).

NEEDLES
One set straight needles size US 10 (6 mm)
One set straight needles size US 11 (8 mm)
One 16" circular (circ) needle size US 10 (6 mm)
Change needle size if necessary to obtain the correct gauge.

NOTIONS
Yarn needle, stitch holders, stitch markers

GAUGE
12 sts and 18 rows = 4" in Stockinette stitch (St st)

BACK
FACING: Using smaller needles and A, CO 60 (66, 72) sts.
Purl 1 row. Knit 2 rows (fold line).

ESTABLISH PATTERN: (RS) Change to larger needles;
k40 (44, 48) (work in St st throughout), place marker (pm),
p20 (22, 24) (work in Rev St st throughout).
Work 1 row even as established.

JOINING ROW: (RS) Fold facing to WS along fold line;
continuing in pattern as established, * work one st from
needle together with one st from CO edge; repeat from *
across. Work even until piece measures 15" from fold line,
ending with a WS row.

SHAPE ARMHOLE: (RS) BO 4 sts at beg of next 2 rows—
52 (58, 64) sts remain. Work even until armhole measures
7 (7½, 8)" from beginning of shaping, ending with a WS row;
pm each side of center 32 (34, 36) sts for neck.

SHAPE NECK: K10 (12, 14); join a second ball of yarn and
BO center sts; work to end. Working both sides at the same
time, work even until armhole measures 7½ (8, 8½)".
BO all sts.

LEFT FRONT

Using smaller needles, CO 26 (29, 32) sts.
Working all sts in St st throughout, work as for Back, working armhole shaping at beginning of RS row, until armhole measures 3 (3½, 4)" from beginning of shaping, ending with a WS row— 22 (25, 28) sts remain.

SHAPE NECK: At neck edge, decrease 1 st every row 12 (13, 14) times as follows:
(RS) Work across to last 3 sts; k2tog, k1.
(WS) Slip 1, p2tog, purl to end—10 (12, 14) sts remain.
Work even until armhole measures same as Back to shoulder. BO rem sts.

RIGHT FRONT

Work as for left Front, reversing shaping; work armhole shaping at beginning of WS rows, neck shaping at beginning of RS rows as follows:
(RS) Slip 1, ssk, knit to end.
(WS) Purl across to last 2 sts, ssp, p1.

RIGHT SLEEVE

Using larger needle and B, CO 28 (30, 32) sts. Knit 2 rows.
Begin St st; work even for 5 rows, ending with a WS row.

SHAPE SLEEVE: (RS) Increase 1 st each side this row, then every 6 rows 10 times—50 (52, 54) sts; and AT THE SAME TIME, when piece measures 2" from the beginning, join A.

ESTABLISH COLOR PATTERN: Continuing Sleeve shaping, * work 1 row A, 4 rows B; repeat from * twice; break B. Change to Rev St st and A only; continuing shaping, work until piece measures 21" from the beginning, ending with a WS row.

SHAPE CAP: (RS) BO 4 sts at beg of next 2 rows—42 (44, 46). Decrease 1 st each side every other row 2 times—38 (40, 42) sts remain. When sleeve measures 22½" from the beginning, BO all sts.

LEFT SLEEVE

Using larger needles and C, CO 28 (30, 32) sts. Knit 2 rows.
Begin St st; working shaping as for right Sleeve, continue with C until piece measures 5¾" from the beginning.
Change to B; work 2 rows.
Change to Rev St st and A; complete left Sleeve as for right Sleeve.

FRONT PANEL/YOKE

Using larger needles and B, CO 10 sts; begin Rev St.
Work even until piece measures 17" from the beginning, ending with a WS row.

SHAPE YOKE: (RS) Increase 1 st each side this row, then every row 13 (14, 15) times—38 (40, 42) sts; pm each side of center 20 sts.

SHAPE NECK: Work across to marker; place center sts on holder for neck; join a second ball of yarn and work to end—9 (10, 11) sts remain each side. Working both sides at same time, work 1 row even. (RS) Decrease 1 st each neck edge once—8 (9, 10) sts remain each side for shoulder. Place sts on holders.

BACK PANEL

Using larger needles and B, CO 38 (40, 42) sts; beg Rev St st.
Work even until piece measures 2" from the beginning, ending with a WS row; pm each side of center 22 sts.

SHAPE NECK: Work across to marker; place center sts on holder for neck; join a second ball of yarn and work to end—8 (9, 10) sts remain each side for shoulder. Working both sides at same time, work even for 2 rows. Leave sts on needle.

SHOULDERS: With RS's facing each other, using 3-needle BO method (see Special Techniques, page 113), join shoulder seams of Back and Front Yoke Panels, leaving 5 sts each side of neck edge on holders for neck.

UNISEX DECONSTRUCTED PULLOVER

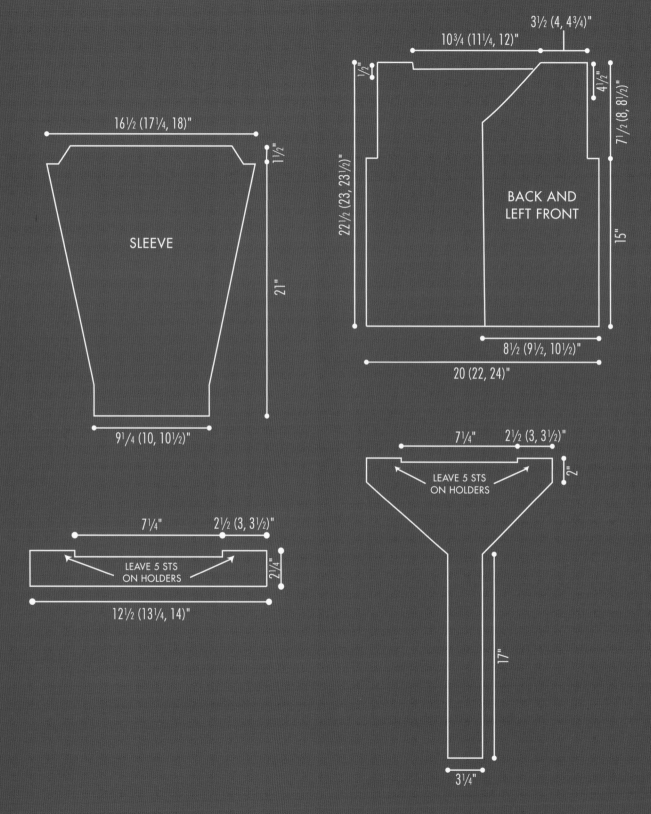

SLEEVE

16½ (17¼, 18)"

1½"

21"

9¼ (10, 10½)"

BACK AND LEFT FRONT

3½ (4, 4¾)"

10¾ (11¼, 12)"

½"

4½"

7½ (8, 8½)"

15"

22½ (23, 23½)"

8½ (9½, 10½)"

20 (22, 24)"

7¼"

2½ (3, 3½)"

LEAVE 5 STS ON HOLDERS

2¼"

12½ (13¼, 14)"

7¼"

2½ (3, 3½)"

2"

LEAVE 5 STS ON HOLDERS

17"

3¼"

FINISHING

Block pieces to measurements.

NECK (YOKE PANEL): With RS facing, using B and circ needle, beginning at Back neck holder, purl 22 sts from holder; purl 10 sts along left shoulder (5 sts left on Back and Front after joining shoulder); purl 20 sts from Front neck holder; purl 10 sts along right shoulder as for left shoulder—62 sts. Join for working in the rnd; pm for beginning of rnd. Begin Rev St st; work even for 3 rnds. Knit 1 rnd, purl 1 rnd. Change to C; knit 1 rnd, then purl 2 rnds. BO all sts in knit.

With WS's facing each other, using yarn needle threaded with A and backstitch or seaming method desired, sew shoulder seams of Back and Fronts. Sew in Sleaves; sew Sleeve and side seams in same manner.

Lay sweater flat so that Front is facing you. Lay Front/Yoke panel into position just inside left and right Front and neck opening. Align lower edge of Front/Yoke with lower edges of left and right Fronts; pin Front/Yoke into place, overlapping Fronts and Front/Yoke approximately 3/8".

Thread yarn needle with C. Beginning at lower left Front edge, attach left Front to Yoke by working a running stitch through both layers; continue up left Front, around neck and down right Front. Weave in loose ends.

[AlterExercise]

INSPIRING WORDS

When you read or hear an idea or quote that inspires you, write it down in your *AlterKnits* notebook. If you like, start with some of the quotes sprinkled throughout this book. Consider writing or embroidering some of these short messages on small pieces of fabric and using them as labels for your handknits. If you write the message, be sure to use a pen specially made for fabric so that the ink won't fade away or bleed when the project is washed. I have also found that a Sharpie marker works.

"NO great discovery
WAS EVER MADE WITHOUT A
bold guess."

— ISAAC NEWTON

Recycled Sweater Totes

·•·

These totes are made from old sweaters THAT ARE FELTED IN THE WASHING MACHINE. YOU CAN CREATE THE HANDLES BY CUTTING THE SWEATER STRATEGICALLY AFTER YOU FELT IT OR YOU CAN TAKE THE FELTED BAG TO A SHOEMAKER OR TAILOR AND ASK HIM OR HER TO ATTACH LEATHER HANDLES FOR YOU. ONCE YOU START MAKING THESE BAGS, I warn you that you may become obsessed WITH FINDING "NEW" SWEATERS TO WORK WITH AT THRIFT STORES, EVEN IN THE DRAWERS OF FAMILY MEMBERS AND FRIENDS.

FINISHED MEASUREMENTS
Sizes will vary. Totes shown are all approximately 16½" wide and vary in height from 12" to 20".

MATERIALS
One 100% wool sweater (NOT machine-washable)
Totes shown made with adult Large sweaters.

NOTIONS
Sewing needle and thread or sewing machine, dressmaker's chalk or quilter's pencil, ruler, scissors, at least 36" long recycled leather belt, strap, or dog leash for handle (if making bag with leather handles)

FELTING
Felt the sweater following the instructions on page 113, noting these changes:
Once sweater is felted sufficiently, if it is machine-knitted, let it run through the spin cycle, then lay flat to dry or put in dryer. If the sweater is hand-knitted, do not run it through the spin cycle or put it in the dryer; lay it flat to dry.

FINISHING BAG WITH FABRIC STRAPS
Lay sweater flat with neck and shoulders closest to you, squaring the bottom. Measure down to just under the armhole; using dressmaker's chalk or quilter's pencil, draw a horizontal line across the body of the sweater for top of Tote.

FABRIC STRAPS: Beginning just to the left of the right sleeve, cutting away sleeve and sleeve seam of sweater, make a vertical cut, through both layers, stopping at the horizontal chalk line at the underarm. Turn scissors making a 90-degree cut to the side seam; discard sleeve. Repeat for left side.

Beginning to the right of the collar/neck edge, make another vertical cut parallel to the first, ending at the same horizontal chalk line. Repeat for left side of collar/neck edge. Cut along the horizontal chalk line, between the last two vertical cuts, removing the center rectangle (collar/neck edge).

SEAMS: Fold sweater so that original side seams are aligned center front and back. Pin bottom of sweater with WS's together. Topstitch (or use a zigzag stitch) a ½" seam along the bottom of the sweater—this is usually the ribbing section. Topstitch along top edge of Tote and Handles. Fold Handles in half, matching up the shoulder seams at the center point, and pin in place. Stitch both sides together 2½" from center down each side—5" total.

POCKET: If desired, use neck section of sweater to create a pocket, as follows: Trim neck section cut away from sweater to measure approximately 5" x 6", preserving ribbing at neck, if desired. Pin pocket into position on one side of Tote, centering it both vertically and horizontally. Topstitch pocket to the Tote, working down one side, across the bottom, and up the other side (leave top open).

FINISHING BAG WITH LEATHER STRAPS
Cut directly across the felted sweater just under the arms. Discard sleeves and upper portion of sweater. Designate the cut edge as the bottom of your Tote. With right sides together, sew bottom of Tote together by hand or by machine. To form bottom and side gussets, arrange the Tote on a flat surface so that the bottom lies flat and you see a triangular "flap" on each side. Sew a short seam across the triangular flap at each side approx 2" in from the point of the triangle. Turn Tote right side out. Cut leather handle material into two 18" pieces. Take the Tote and leather to a shoemaker or tailor and ask him or her to attach securely.

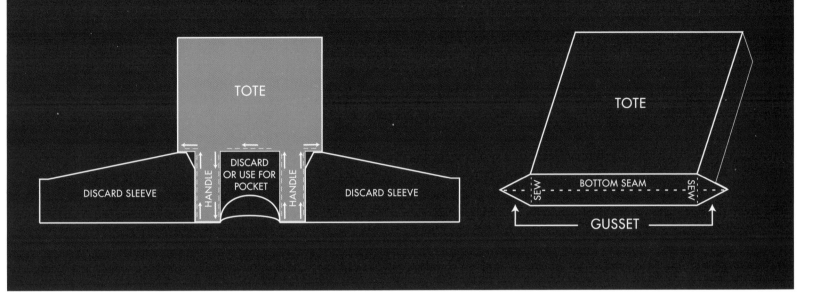

TOTE WITH FABRIC STRAPS

TOTE

DISCARD SLEEVE

HANDLE

DISCARD OR USE FOR POCKET

HANDLE

DISCARD SLEEVE

TOTE WITH LEATHER STRAPS

TOTE

SEW

BOTTOM SEAM

SEW

GUSSET

[AlterExercise]
GIVE IT A CHANCE

This exercise works best in a group. It is meant to help us overcome our
resistance to doing certain types of knitting.

TO GET READY
Put small balls of different kinds of yarn and an assortment of knitting needles in the center of a table
(make sure that you have about twice as many balls of yarn as you have people
participating in this exercise so there's a lot of yarn to choose from). Place a few knitting
reference books and stitch dictionaries on the table.

TO START
Ask each knitter to choose a ball of yarn she or he likes. Then ask each knitter to work a swatch
using a stitch pattern or technique that she or he finds difficult or doesn't like to do
(refer to reference books and stitch dictionaries, as necessary). After knitting for awhile, talk about
the experience. The idea is to help one another overcome challenges and blocks or possibly
find the appeal in what was previously avoided.

Stash Bags

· · ·

THESE BAGS ARE A fun and useful way to use up stash yarn. THE BAG IS KNITTED IN STRIPES IN THE ROUND, THEN THE BOTTOM IS SEWN UP AND THE BAG IS FELTED. KNITTED HANDLES CAN BE ADDED BEFORE FELTING, BUT I ACTUALLY PREFER TO CREATE HANDLES WITH TRANSPARENT PLASTIC TUBING FROM THE HARDWARE STORE. TO personalize the bags, I WRITE OR STAMP inspirational words or messages ON RIBBON AND SLIP THE RIBBON INTO THE TUBING.

FINISHED MEASUREMENTS
MEDIUM: 19" x 26" before felting; 17½" x 15½" after felting
LARGE: 22" x 35" before felting; 20" x 20" after felting

YARN
Assortment of mostly worsted-weight yarn from your personal stash (NOT machine-washable). Approximately 900 yards total for medium bag and 1250 yards total for large bag.

Note: The bulk of yarns used for these bags are worsted weight. It is fine to incorporate lighter-or heavier-weight yarns into your color and yarn sequence, but keep in mind this will make the diameter of the bag slightly different in the sections where this yarn is used. If you plan to knit the bulk of your bag with worsted-weight yarn, limit the number of rounds you knit with yarns of other weights to six at a time and always intersperse the variant-weight yarn in between sections of worsted-weight yarn. You can also use double or triple strands of a lighter-weight yarn in order to match the gauge of your worsted-weight yarn. Once the tote is felted, the worsted-weight yarn surrounding your variant yarn will help keep your tote the size you had intended.

Novelty yarns are another great addition to this project. Again, be sure you place your novelty (non-felting) yarns in between multiple rows of wool yarn that will felt.

NEEDLES
One 29" circular (circ) needle size US 10½ (6.5 mm)
Two double-pointed needles (dpn) size US 10½ (6.5 mm)
Change needle size if necessary to obtain the correct gauge.

NOTIONS
Yarn needle, stitch marker
Optional (for handle): About 3 feet transparent plastic water-pressure tubing, two 17"-long pieces wide double-fold bias tape or ribbon, fabric marker or rubber stamps/ink, sharp tapestry needle, embroidery floss, 4 (about 1¼") buttons, hole puncher

GAUGE
14 sts and 18 rows = 4" in Stockinette stitch (St st) before felting

BAG

Using color of choice, CO 125 (150) sts. Join for working in the rnd, being careful not to twist sts; place marker (pm) for beginning of rnd. Begin St st; work even, changing yarns as desired, until the Bag measures 26 (35)" from the beginning. BO all sts.

FINISHING

With RS's together, using yarn threaded onto yarn needle, sew the bottom seam. Turn Bag inside out and flatten the bottom as shown in diagram at right. Sew a short seam across the triangular flap at each side approx 3½ (4¾)" from end of each triangle point, to form bottom and side gussets for Bag. Weave in loose ends.

KNITTED HANDLES (make 2—work before Bag is felted)

Lay Bag flat and mark top of Bag for handle position— approximately 6½" in from right and left sides. Using dpn, pick up 7 sts at handle position, working towards the center on the right-hand side of the Bag. Using 2 dpn and 2 strands of yarn, work as follows: * K4, yf, sl 3, turn; repeat from * until handle measures 15" in length.
BO all sts, leaving a 10"-long tail. Thread tail onto yarn needle and sew end of handle where marked on the left-hand side, on the same side of Bag.
Repeat for second handle, on opposite side of Bag.

FELTING

Felt Bag following the instructions on page 113.

PLASTIC HANDLES (attach after Bag is felted)

Lay Bag flat and mark top of Bag for handle position— approximately 7½" in from right-hand and left-hand sides of Bag. Cut 2 lengths of bias tape/ribbon, each 17" long; write or stamp inspirational words onto bias tape/ribbon. Let dry completely. Turn and stamp other side, if desired.

Cut 2 lengths of plastic tubing approximately 18" long. Punch 2 holes side-by-side at each end of tubing. Beginning on the right-hand side of Bag, thread sharp tapestry needle with embroidery floss and sew up through Bag and hole punched into end of plastic. Thread through a button and back down through second hole punched into plastic and through felted Bag.
Repeat several times until handle is secure.

Insert stamped bias tape/ribbon through center of tubing; secure opposite end of handle to left-hand side of Bag.

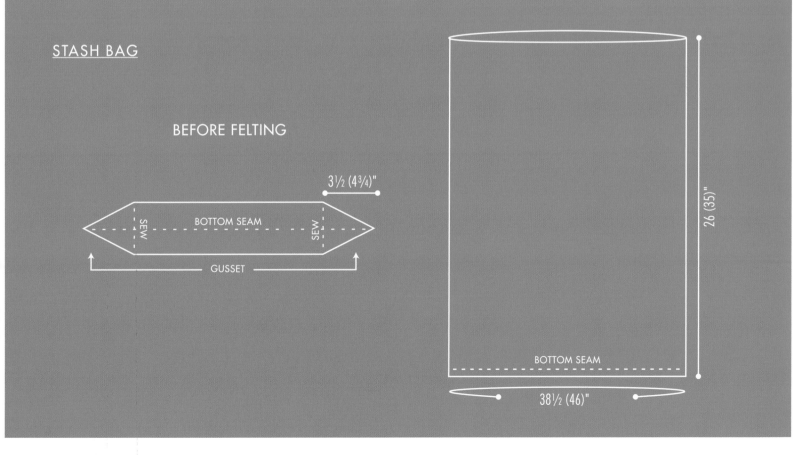

STASH BAG

BEFORE FELTING

3¹⁄₂ (4³⁄₄)"

SEW   BOTTOM SEAM   SEW

GUSSET

26 (35)"

BOTTOM SEAM

38¹⁄₂ (46)"

"THE impossible IS OFTEN THE untried."

—JIM GOODWIN

Screen Door

— • —

Once I decided I wanted to take on the challenge OF KNITTING A SCREEN FOR A DOOR, I SWATCHED WITH AN ARRAY OF MATERIALS. I KNEW I NEEDED SOMETHING FLEXIBLE AND DURABLE AND ABLE TO WITHSTAND OUTDOOR WEATHER CONDITIONS. I TRIED craft wire, fishing line, sewing thread, AND nylon rope, AMONG OTHER MATERIALS, UNTIL I FINALLY SETTLED ON UV-coated nylon upholstery thread. DOUBLE-STRANDED AND WORKED IN GARTER STITCH, THIS KIND OF THREAD IS INCREDIBLY FLEXIBLE AND SPRINGY AND GIVES THE SCREEN A VERY INTERESTING LOOK, more unique than you might expect from such a humble medium. THESE INSTRUCTIONS ARE WRITTEN FOR THE SIZE DOOR FRAME I USED. IF YOUR DOOR FRAME IS A DIFFERENT SIZE, YOU'LL NEED TO KNIT A SWATCH AND RECALCULATE THE NUMBER OF STITCHES YOU NEED TO CAST ON TO ACHEIVE THE MEASUREMENTS DESIRED. YOUR KNITTED SCREEN SHOULD MEASURE FIVE TO TEN PERCENT SMALLER THAN THE OPENING IN THE DOOR FRAME, DEPENDING ON HOW TAUT YOU WANT THE SCREEN TO BE ONCE IT IS MOUNTED.

FINISHED MEASUREMENTS
23" x 57" (unstretched)

YARN
Ultra Dee UV-Coated Nylon Upholstery Thread (100% bonded polyester; 1035 yards): 2 spools. Shown in #1412 bird's egg blue (see Sources for Supplies, page 118).

NEEDLES
One set straight needles size US 8 (5 mm)
Change needle size if necessary to obtain the correct gauge.

MATERIALS
Recycled wooden screen door (shown with opening 23¾" x 59¾"), wood molding cut to dimensions of door opening (with ends cut at 45-degree angles); heavy-duty staple gun, ¼" staples, finishing nails

GAUGE
18 sts and 44 rows = 4" in Garter stitch

SCREEN
With 2 strands of thread held together, CO 103 sts; begin Garter st. Work even until piece measures 57" from the beginning. BO all sts loosely.

ASSEMBLY
Lay door on a flat surface. Mark the horizontal and vertical centers of the opening with a pencil.

Lay knitted screen over the door opening. Beginning with the upper right-hand corner of the screen, staple the knitted screen to the upper right-hand corner of the door opening.

Note: You want to staple your work fairly close to the edge of the opening (approximately ½"); it will be covered by molding after the entire screen is stapled in place.

Once the upper right-hand corner is secure, staple the lower left-hand corner of the screen to the lower left-hand corner of the door opening, stretching the screen firmly into place; repeat for remaining 2 corners.

When all four corners are securely stapled, staple the vertical right-hand center of screen to the vertical right-hand center of the door opening; repeat for the left-hand side, then the center top and bottom.

Continue stapling the screen into place, alternating side to side and top to bottom; this will ensure that your screen is evenly placed within the door opening. Place staples as closely as possible, to ensure that screen is evenly stretched in opening.

When the screen has been stapled securely into the door opening, nail molding into place, covering edges of screen.

[AlterExercise]
GUARANTEED SUCCESS!

In your *AlterKnits* notebook, write down your answer to the following question:

WHAT WOULD YOU ATTEMPT TO KNIT IF YOU WERE GUARANTEED NOT TO FAIL?

Once you've finished, look over your list. Is there anything listed here that you feel ready to try?

Is your local yarn shop or guild offering a class covering any of these techniques? Could one of your friends teach you any of them?

"I CAN create
WHAT I CAN imagine."
—CHARLENE KINGSTON

Decoupage Dress Form

What to do with all of those yarn labels? COLLECT THEM AND USE THEM TO DECOUPAGE A DRESS FORM OR ANY SURFACE, SUCH AS A HATBOX OR EVEN A TABLE OR SMALL DRESSER. IF YOU ARE eager to decoupage BUT DON'T HAVE ENOUGH LABELS FOR YOUR PROJECT, ASK FRIENDS, PUT UP A SIGN AT A LOCAL YARN SHOP, OR EVEN POST A MESSAGE ON THE INTERNET. IMAGINE HOW INTERESTING IT COULD BE TO collect labels from around the world. FOR THE DRESS FORM SHOWN, WHICH IS 26" TALL AND WHOSE MEASUREMENTS ARE 32" (CHEST), 25" (WAIST), AND 34" (HIPS), I USED APPROXIMATELY 250 LABELS.

MATERIALS
Dress form, yarn labels, 8 ounces Mod Podge Matte (or Elmer's Glue-All), shallow bowl or foil pie tin, 12-ounce can spray-on polyurethane

DECOUPAGE
Combine a 50/50 mixture of Mod Podge and water in bowl or pie tin.

One at a time, dip yarn labels into Mod Podge-water mixture to soften (see Decoupage Tips at right).

With your fingers, wipe away excess glue from the labels and position labels onto dress form in a random pattern. Continue gluing labels to dress form, overlapping labels, until it is entirely covered.

Once all of the labels are in place and the glue is dry, in a well-ventilated area, spray the dress form with an even layer of polyurethane following the instructions on the can. Let dry for several hours. Spray 1 or 2 more coats, as desired. The more coats you put on, the more protected the piece will be against water or abrasion.

DECOUPAGE TIPS
The longer you leave your label in the glue mixture, the softer the label will become. This also means the paper is breaking down, so be careful not to leave it in too long, or the label will fall apart. Some labels will be soft enough to use in 10 to 15 seconds so begin with that; labels constructed of very heavy paper may need to soak for a minute or two.

For the curved areas, choose smaller pieces (cutting or tearing labels to desired size if needed) and layer them following the curve. You may also want to make a few ¼" cuts on one side of the label; this makes the label easier to manipulate so it will cover the curved area.

[SPECIAL TECHNIQUES]

FOLLOWING ARE INSTRUCTIONS FOR SPECIAL TECHNIQUES CALLED FOR IN THE PATTERNS IN THIS BOOK. FOR ADDITIONAL TECHNICAL INSTRUCTION, SEE THE BOOKS LISTED IN THE BIBLIOGRAPHY ON PAGE 120.

3-NEEDLE BO METHOD: Place the stitches to be joined onto two same-size needles; hold the pieces to be joined with the right sides facing each other and the needles parallel, pointing in the same direction (to the right). Holding both needles in your left hand, using the working yarn and a third needle the same size or one size larger, insert the third needle into the first stitch on the front needle, then into the first stitch on the back needle; knit these two sts together; * knit the next stitch from each needle together (two stitches on the right-hand needle); pass the first stitch over the second stitch to BO one stitch. Repeat from * until one stitch remains on the third needle; cut the yarn and fasten off.

DOUBLE CROCHET (dc): Working from right to left, yarn over the hook (2 loops on hook), insert the hook into the next stitch, yarn over the hook and pull up a loop (3 loops on hook), [yarn over and draw through 2 loops] twice.

DUPLICATE STITCH: This technique is similar to Kitchener stitch, except that it's used for decorative purposes instead of joining two pieces together.

Thread a yarn needle with chosen yarn, leaving a tail to be woven in later; * bring the needle from the WS to the RS of the piece at the base of the stitch to be covered, pull the yarn through to the RS; pass the needle under both loops of the base of the stitch above the stitch to be covered; insert the needle into the same place where you started (at the base of the stitch being covered), and pull the yarn through to the WS of the piece. Be sure that the new stitch is the same

tension as the rest of the piece. Repeat from * for additional stitches, carrying the yarn loosely across the WS of the piece.

A good way to visualize the path of the yarn for Duplicate stitch is to work a swatch in Stockinette stitch using the main color (MC) for three rows; work one row alternating MC and a contrasting color, then work two additional rows using the MC only.

EDGE STITCHES: Slip the first stitch knitwise on every row, and knit or purl (as specified in the instructions) the last stitch.

FELTING: Fill washing machine with hot water (lowest water level possible) and add 1–2 tablespoons dishwashing soap. Place the piece to be felted into the washing machine; set machine to agitate. Check progress every few minutes. Felting time will vary based on the temperature and type of water, as well as the type of soap used and the intensity of agitation; it may take several cycles. Felt projects in this book until knitted stitches are no longer visible and you have a smooth impermeable fabric.

* Do not let the piece run through the spin cycle; doing so may cause permanent creases. Remove the piece and roll in dry towel to remove excess water; lay flat to air-dry, checking on piece periodically and reshaping as needed; it may take several days to fully dry.

* Felting may vary based on specific needs of project so read instructions carefully before beginning.

[SPECIAL TECHNIQUES, CONTINUED]

GARTER STITCH: Knit every row when working straight (in rows); knit 1 round, purl 1 round when working in the round.

GRAFT STITCHES (KITCHENER STITCH): Using a yarn needle, thread a length of yarn approximately 4 times the length of the section to be joined. Hold the pieces to be joined wrong sides together, with the needles holding the stitches parallel, both ends pointing in the same direction. Working from right to left, *insert the yarn needle into the first stitch on the front needle as if to knit, pull the yarn through, remove the stitch from the front needle; insert the yarn needle into the next stitch on the front needle as if to purl, pull the yarn through, leave the stitch on front needle; insert the yarn needle into the first stitch on the back needle as if to purl, pull the yarn through, remove the stitch from the back needle; insert the yarn needle into the next stitch on the back needle as if to knit, pull the yarn through, leave the stitch on back needle. Repeat from *, working 3 or 4 stitches at a time, then go back and adjust the tension to match the pieces being joined. When 1 stitch remains on each needle, cut the yarn and fasten off.

HALF-HITCH (SEWN) BO: This BO technique is very flexible and creates an edge that closely resembles the Long-Tail (thumb) CO. Each stitch is worked through twice, once knitwise and once purlwise. Using a yarn needle, thread a length of yarn approximately 4 times the length of the section to be bound off.

With RS facing, * insert the yarn needle into the second stitch on the left-hand needle knitwise, and pull yarn through; adjust the tension of the yarn so that the first 2 stitches on the left-hand needle are held together at the same tension as the fabric of the piece; insert the yarn needle into the first stitch purlwise, pull the yarn through and adjust tension; drop the first stitch from the left-hand needle; repeat from * across.

I-CORD: Using a double-pointed needle (dpn), cast on or pick up the required number of stitches; * without turning the dpn, slide the stitches to the other end of the needle, pull the yarn snuggly around the back (WS), and knit the stitches. Repeat from * until the cord is the length desired.
Note: After a few rows, the tubular shape will become apparent.

LONG-TAIL (THUMB) CO: Leaving a tail with about 1" of yarn for each stitch to be cast-on, make a slipknot in the yarn and place it on the right-hand needle; insert the thumb and forefinger of your left hand between the strands of yarn so that the working end is around your forefinger, and the tail end is around your thumb, "slingshot" fashion.

* Insert the tip of the right-hand needle into the front loop on the thumb, hook the strand of yarn coming from the forefinger from back to front, and draw it through the loop on your thumb; remove your thumb from the loop; pull on the working yarn to tighten the new stitch on the right-hand needle; return your thumb and forefinger to their original positions. Repeat from * for the remaining stitches to be CO.

MAKE ONE (M1 OR M1-L——LEFT-SLANTING INCREASE): With the tip of the left-hand needle inserted from front to back, lift the strand between the two needles onto the left-hand needle; knit the strand through the back loop, twisting the stitch, to increase one stitch.

M1-R (RIGHT-SLANTING INCREASE): With the tip of the left-hand needle inserted from back to front, lift the strand between the two needles onto the left-hand needle; knit it through the front loop, twisting the stitch, to increase one stitch.

READING CHARTS: Unless otherwise specified in the instructions, charts are read from right to left for RS rows, from left to right for WS rows when working straight (in rows); the numbers will indicate whether the chart begins with a RS or WS row. All rounds are read from right to left when working circular (in the round).

REVERSE STOCKINETTE STITCH (Rev St st): Purl the RS rows, knit the WS rows when working straight (in rows); purl every round when working circular (in the round).

RIBBING: Although Rib stitch patterns use different numbers of stitches, all are worked in the same way, whether straight (in rows) or circular. The instructions will specify how many stitches to knit or purl; the example below uses k1, p1 rib.

Row/Rnd 1: * K1, p1; repeat from * across (end k1 if an odd number of stitches).

Row/Rnd 2: Knit the knit stitches and purl the purl stitches as they face you.

Repeat Row/Rnd 2 for Rib st.

SEED STITCH: Row/Rnd 1:* K1, p1; repeat from * across (end k1 if an odd number of stitches).

Row/Rnd 2: Knit the purls and purl the knits as they face you.

Repeat Row/Rnd 2 for Seed st.

SHORT ROW SHAPING: Work the number of stitches specified in the instructions, wrap and turn (wrp-t) as follows:

(WS) Work across to specified number of stitches before the end of the row: Bring the yarn to the back of the piece—knit position (yb), slip the next stitch purlwise to the right-hand needle (slip 1), bring the yarn forward to the front of the piece—purl position (yf), return the slipped stitch to the left-hand needle, turn, ready to work the next row, leaving remaining stitches unworked—the slipped stitch has been wrapped.

(RS) Work across to specified number of stitches before the end of the row: Bring the yarn forward to the front of the piece—purl position (yf), slip the next stitch purlwise to the right-hand needle (slip 1), bring the yarn to the back of the piece—knit position (yb), return the slipped stitch to the left-hand needle, turn, ready to work the next row, leaving remaining stitches unworked—the slipped stitch has been wrapped.

When the Short Rows are completed, or when working progressively longer Short Rows, work the wrap together with the wrapped stitch as you come to it, as follows:

(RS) If the stitch to be worked is a knit stitch, insert the right-hand needle into the wrap (from beneath the wrap up), then into the wrapped stitch knitwise, k2tog (the wrap and the wrapped stitch).

(WS) If the stitch to be worked is a purl stitch, insert the right-hand needle into the wrapped stitch purlwise, then into the wrap (from above the wrap down), p2tog (the wrap and the wrapped stitch).

Note: Wrap may be lifted onto the left-hand needle, then worked together with the wrapped stitch if this is more convenient.

SINGLE CROCHET (sc): Insert the hook into the next stitch and draw up a loop (2 loops on the hook), yarn over and draw through both loops on the hook.

SLIP (KNITTING): Slip all stitches purlwise unless otherwise instructed.

SLIP STITCH (CROCHET) (sl st): Insert the hook in the next stitch (or stitch specified in the instructions), yarn over the hook and draw through the loop on the hook.

STOCKINETTE STITCH (St st): Knit the RS rows, purl the WS rows when working straight (in rows); knit every round when working circular (in the round).

TRIPLE CROCHET (Tr): Working from right to left, yarn over the hook twice (3 loops on hook), insert hook into next stitch, yarn over the hook and pull up a loop (4 loops on hook), [yarn over and draw through 2 loops] 3 times.

YARN OVER (yo): Bring the yarn forward to the purl position, then place it in position to work the next stitch. If the next stitch is to be knit, bring the yarn over the needle, knit the next stitch. If the next stitch is to be purled, bring the yarn over the needle, then forward again to the purl position, purl the next stitch. On the next row, unless instructed otherwise, work the yarn over through the front loop, in the Stitch pattern for that row, forming an eyelet.

[ABBREVIATIONS]

BO :   bind off

Ch: chain

Circ: circular

CO: cast on

Dc: double crochet

Dpn: double-pointed needles

K: knit

K1-f/b: knit into the front and back loop of the next
stitch to increase one stitch.

K2tog: knit 2 stitches together (single decrease)

M1:   make 1 (see Special Techniques, page 114)

M1-L: make 1 (left-slanting increase)

M1-R: make 1 (right-slanting increase)

P :   purl

P2tog: purl 2 stitches together (single decrease)

Pm :   place a marker

Psso :   pass slipped stitch over

Rnd :   round

RS :   right side

Sc :   single crochet (see Special Techniques, page 115)

Skp :   slip next stitch knitwise, k1, psso (single decrease)

Sk2p :   slip next stitch knitwise, k2tog, psso
(double decrease)

Sp2p :   slip next st purlwise, p2tog, psso (double decrease)

Sl st :   slip stitch (crochet)

Sm :   slip marker

Ssk: slip the next 2 stitches, one at a time knitwise,
to the right-hand needle, return the 2 stitches to
left-hand needle in turned position, k2tog-tbl.

Ssp :   slip the next 2 stitches, one at a time knitwise,
to the right-hand needle, return the 2 stitches to the
left-hand needle in turned position, p2tog-tbl.

St(s) :   stitch(es)

Tbl :   through the back loop(s)

Tr: triple crochet

Wrp-t :   wrap and turn (see Special Technique—
Short Row Shaping, page 115)

WS :   wrong side

Wyib :   with yarn in back

Wyif :   with yarn in front

Yb :   yarn back

Yf :   yarn forward

Yo :   yarn over (see Special Techniques, page 115)

[SOURCES *for* SUPPLIES]

RECYCLED BUILDING
MATERIALS

THE REBUILDING CENTER
3625 N. Mississippi Avenue
Portland, OR 97227
503.331.1877
www.rebuildingcenter.org

REJUVENATION INC.
1100 SE Grand Avenue
Portland, OR 97214
888.401.1900
www.rejunvenation.com

RECYCLED FURNITURE
FLEA
4419 NE Fremont Street
Portland, OR 97213
503.282.0508

VESTIGES ANTIQUES & COLLECTIBLES
4743 NE Fremont Street
Portland, OR 97213
503.331.3920

LEATHER LACING
OREGON LEATHER COMPANY
110 NW Second Avenue
Portland, OR 97209
503.228.4105

BEADS
DAVA BEAD AND TRADE
1815 NE Broadway
Portland, OR 97232
877.962.3282
www.davabeadandtrade.com

BUTTONS, RIBBON
THE BUTTON EMPORIUM
914 SW 11th Avenue
Portland, OR 97205
503.228.6372
www.buttonemporium.com

RIBBON &
HANDMADE PAPERS
ARTEMIS EXQUISITE
EMBELLISHMENTS
5155 Myrtle Avenue
Eureka, CA 95503
888.233.5187
www.artemisinc.com

KATE'S PAPERIE
8 West 13th Street
New York, NY 10011
212.633.0570
www.katespaperie.com

THE PAPER ZONE
1136 SE Grand Avenue
Portland, OR 97214
503.233.2933
www.paperzone.com

OBLATION PAPERS & PRESS
516 NW 12th Avenue
Portland, OR 97209
503.223.1093
www.oblationpapers.com

FABRIC
JOSEPHINE'S DRY GOODS
521 SW 11th Avenue
Portland, OR 97205
503.224.4202
www.josephinesdrygoods.com

FABRIC DEPOT
700 NE 122nd Avenue
Portland, OR 97233
888.896.1478
www.fabricdepot.com

THE WHOLE 9 YARDS
1033 NW Glisan
Portland, OR 97209
503.223.2880
www.w9yards.com

UPHOLSTERY THREAD
HOCH & SELBY
809 NE 25th Avenue
Portland, OR 97232
800.659.9904

FABRIC PAINT & SPONGES
MICHAEL'S, THE ARTS AND
CRAFTS STORE
www.michaels.com

KNITTING NEEDLES
LANTERN MOON
(wholesale only; contact or check
website to locate a retailer near you)
800.530.4170
www.lanternmoon.com

DRESS FORMS

GRAND & BENEDICTS USED ANNEX
122 SE Morrison Street
Portland, OR 97214
503.234.3792
www.grand-benedicts.com

RECYCLED SWEATERS &
T-SHIRTS
GOODWILL INDUSTRIES
301.530.6500
www.goodwill.org

YARN

BLUE SKY ALPACAS
PO Box 387
St. Francis, MN 55070
888.460.8862
www.blueskyalpacas.com

BROWN SHEEP COMPANY
100662 County Road 16
Mitchell, NE 69357
800.826.9136
www.brownsheep.com

CASCADE YARNS
1224 Andover Park E
Tukwila, WA 98188
800.548.1048
www.cascadeyarns.com

CLASSIC ELITE YARNS
122 Western Avenue
Lowell, MA 01851
800.444.5648
www.classiceliteyarns.com

DESIGN SOURCE
(MANOS DEL URUGUAY)
38 Montvale Avenue, Suite 145
Stoneham, MA 02180
781.438.9631

FIESTA YARNS
5401 San Diego Drive NE
Albuquerque, NM 87113
505.892.5008
www.fiestayarns.com

HABU TEXTILES
135 West 29th Street, Suite 804
New York, NY 10001
212.239.3546
www.habutextiles.com

LOUET SALES
808 Commerce Park Drive
Ogdensburg, NY 13669
613.925.4502
www.louet.com

MUENCH YARNS
1323 Scott Street
Petaluma, CA 94954
800.733.9276
www.muenchyarns.com

PLYMOUTH YARN COMPANY
PO Box 28
Bristol, PA 19007
215.788.0459
www.plymouthyarn.com

S. R KERTZER LIMITED
50 Trowers Road
Woodbridge, Ontario
L4L 7KS
Canada
800.263.2354
www.kertzer.com

WESTMINSTER FIBERS, INC. (ROWAN)
4 Townsend West, Unit 8
Nashua, NH 03063
800.445.9276

CLOTHING

SEAPLANE
827 NW 23rd
Portland, OR 97210
503.234.2409
www.e-seaplane.com

*All clothing listed below from Seaplane
unless marked with an *.*

Page 10: top by Linea
Page 20: skirt by Frocky Jack Morgan
Page 26: skirt by Linea
Pages 28 and 31: dress by Kathryn
Towers and man's jacket by DSR
Page 44: skirt by Claire la Faye
*Page 48: dress by Jamie Guinn
*Pages 60 and 63: dress by Jamie Guinn
Page 86: dress by Kathryn Towers

[BIBLIOGRAPHY]

THE FOLLOWING LIST INCLUDES BOOKS
I REFERRED TO WHILE WORKING ON
ALTERKNITS, PLUS SOME OTHERS
THAT CONTINUE TO INSPIRE AND
INSTRUCT ME.

REFERENCE

BUDD, ANN
The Knitter's Handy Book of Patterns,
Interweave Press, 2002.

BUDD, ANN
*The Knitter's Handy Book of Sweater
Patterns*, Interweave Press, 2004.

GALESKAS, BEVERLY
Felted Knits,
Interweave Press, 2003.

HIATT, JUNE HEMMONS
The Principles of Knitting,
Simon & Schuster, 1988.

STANLEY, MONTSE
Reader's Digest Knitter's Handbook,
Reader's Digest, 1993.

WALKER, BARBARA G.
A Treasury of Knitting Patterns,
Schoolhouse Press, 1998.

KNITTING & EMBROIDERY INSPIRATION

CORNELL, KARI
For the Love of Knitting,
Voyageur Press, 2004.

EMBROIDERERS' GUILD
*Embroidery Studio: The Ultimate
Workshop*, David & Charles Books/
EG Enterprises, 1993.

FALICK, MELANIE
Knitting in America, Artisan, 1996.

HISDAL, SOLVEIG, *Poetry in Stitches*,
Damm & Son AS, 2000.

NORSK STRIKKEDESIGN
*A Collection from Norway's Foremost
Knitting Designers*, Unicorn, 2002.

PHILLIPS, MARY WALKER
Creative Knitting
Van Norstrand Reinhold, 1971.

COLOR & PATTERN

ALBERS, JOSEF
Interaction of Color,
Yale University Press, 1963.

BEYER, JINNY
Designing Tessellations,
Contemporary Books, 1999.

BOTHWELL, DORR AND MARLYS
MAYFIELD
*Notan: The Dark-Light Principle of
Design*, Dover Publications, 1991.

COLE, DRUSILLA
1000 Patterns,
Chronicle Books, 2003.

FINLAY, VICTORIA
Color: A Natural History of the Palette,
Random House, 2002.

GUILD, TRICIA
Tricia Guild on Color, Rizzoli, 1993.

CREATIVE INSPIRATION

CAMERON, JULIA
*The Artist's Way: A Spiritual Path
to Higher Creativity*,
Tarcher/Putnam, 1995.

KANDINSKY, WASSILY
Concerning the Spiritual in Art,
Dover, 1977.

MCMILLAN, MICHAEL
*Paper Airplane: A Lesson for Flying
Outside the Box*,
Simon & Schuster, 2004.

SMITH, KERI
*Living Out Loud: Activities to Fuel a
Creative Life*, Chronicle, 2003.

[ACKNOWLEDGEMENTS]

I AM GRATEFUL TO THE FOLLOWING PEOPLE WHO CONTRIBUTED THEIR TIME AND TALENTS TO ALTERKNITS: Melanie Falick, MY EDITOR, FOR TAKING THIS PROJECT UNDER HER WING AND FOR CONTINUING TO INSPIRE ME TO DO MY BEST WORK; EVERYONE WHO WORKED ON THE PHOTOGRAPHY, ESPECIALLY Rebecca Emery, Jay Lawrence, Tavia Onstad, AND Darcy Henderson; PLUS THE MODELS: Ayanna Beaudoin, Chris Becker, Anna Ford, Teisha Helgerson, Brendan Howe, Gabriell Johnston, Glady Lee, Dora Papay, Katya Pearl, Sam Tenenbaum, Kate Towers, Julia Van Riper, Robin Ward, Sally Woodcock, AND Dylan Zerges. FOR GRACIOUSLY WELCOMING US INTO THEIR LIVING AND WORK SPACES FOR PHOTOGRAPHY I MUST THANK Kristin Ford OF FORD FARMS, Kate Sokoloff, Linda Wizner, Todd Leninger, Cathedral Park Studios, AND Oblation Papers & Press. FOR LOANING US THEIR ORIGINAL DRESS DESIGNS FOR PHOTOGRAPHY, THANKS TO Kate Towers OF SEAPLANE AND Jamie Guinn.

SPECIAL THANKS TO THE KNITTERS WHO HELPED IN THE PRODUCTION OF ALTERKNITS: Jesse Stenberg, WHO HAS PROVEN ONCE AGAIN THAT HE IS TRULY "BORN TO KNIT," Lynn Gates, Lucinda Bingham, Sandy Bingham, AND Kate Sokoloff. I AM ALSO INDEBTED TO THE MULTITALENTED TEXTILE GURU Jamie Guinn FOR HER MANY CONTRIBUTIONS TO THESE PROJECTS; TO my dad, Ken Radford, WHOSE CARPENTRY EXPERTISE HELPED TO CREATE A BEAUTIFUL SCREEN DOOR; TO Dee Neer FOR EDITING MY PATTERNS SO CAREFULLY; AND Diane Shaw AND Kathryn Hammill OF GOODESIGN FOR DESIGNING SUCH A BEAUTIFUL BOOK.

I'D ALSO LIKE TO EXPRESS MY GRATITUDE TO Linda Carter OF YARN GARDEN AND Melissa Nelson OF LINT, BOTH IN PORTLAND, OREGON, AND Marilyn Murphy AND Linda Stark OF INTERWEAVE PRESS. I MUST ALSO THANK THE FOLLOWING YARN COMPANIES WHO SO GENEROUSLY PROVIDED YARN FOR THE PROJECTS: BLUE SKY ALPACAS, BROWN SHEEP COMPANY, CASCADE YARNS, CLASSIC ELITE YARNS, DESIGN SOURCE, FIESTA YARNS, HABU TEXTILES, LOUET SALES, MUENCH YARNS & BUTTONS, PLYMOUTH YARN COMPANY, S.R. KERTZER, AND WESTMINSTER FIBERS.

SPECIAL THANKS TO MY FAMILY—Dad, Carol, AND Matt. AND TO MY FRIENDS Kim Demus, Pam Gaier, Linda Lee, MaryBeth Lynn, Deb Parsons, Kristin Spurkland, Sue Stahl, Dawn Witherspoon, AND Sharon Woodcock—YOU CONTINUE TO INSPIRE ME WITH YOUR STRENGTH, CREATIVITY, BEAUTY, AND FRIENDSHIP.

[INDEX]

Povy Kendal Achison

Leigh Radford IS THE ART DIRECTOR OF INTERWEAVE KNITS MAGAZINE AND AN AWARD-WINNING GRAPHIC DESIGNER WITH OVER TWENTY YEARS OF EXPERIENCE IN GRAPHIC DESIGN AND CORPORATE MARKETING. A PASSIONATE, LIFELONG KNITTER, SHE DESIGNS KNITWEAR FOR INTERWEAVE KNITS AS WELL AS FOR KNITTING PATTERN AND YARN COMPANIES. HER WORK ALSO APPEARS IN WEEKEND KNITTING AND HANDKNIT HOLIDAYS (BOTH FROM STEWART, TABORI & CHANG) AND IN SCARF STYLE (INTERWEAVE PRESS). SHE LIVES IN PORTLAND, OREGON.

How does it work?

The **ThomsonNOW** system is made up of three powerful, easy-to-use assessment components:

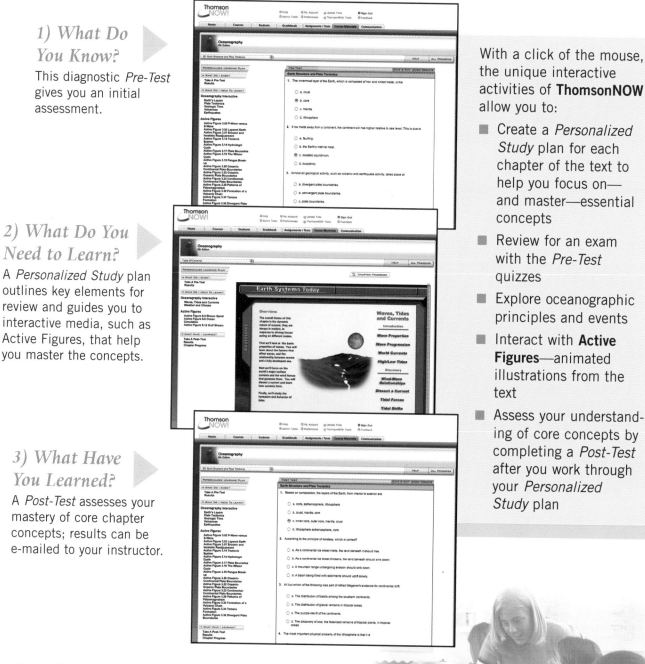

1) *What Do You Know?*

This diagnostic *Pre-Test* gives you an initial assessment.

2) *What Do You Need to Learn?*

A *Personalized Study* plan outlines key elements for review and guides you to interactive media, such as Active Figures, that help you master the concepts.

3) *What Have You Learned?*

A *Post-Test* assesses your mastery of core chapter concepts; results can be e-mailed to your instructor.

With a click of the mouse, the unique interactive activities of **ThomsonNOW** allow you to:

- Create a *Personalized Study* plan for each chapter of the text to help you focus on—and master—essential concepts
- Review for an exam with the *Pre-Test* quizzes
- Explore oceanographic principles and events
- Interact with **Active Figures**—animated illustrations from the text
- Assess your understanding of core concepts by completing a *Post-Test* after you work through your *Personalized Study* plan

Study smarter—and make every minute count!

*If an access card came with your text, you can login to **ThomsonNOW** today by using the URL and code on the card, or purchase access online at*

www.thomsonedu.com